"In this helpful book, Jacob Shatzer
Christian ethic must be tethered to
grounding biblical ethics in biblical theology, he demonstrates that the coherence of the former is reinforced by the narrative beats of the latter. *Biblical Ethics* will be a great foundational resource for pastors and students, as well as a welcome reminder to more seasoned ethicists."

—**Nathan A. Finn**, provost and dean of university faculty, North Greenville University

"A cohesive and comprehensive moral framework may be among the greatest opportunities for reaching a generation that is far from God. Gone are the days when plucking isolated Bible verses in response to isolated issues will satisfy the intellectually inquisitive mind. Dr. Shatzer invites us to build our Christian ethics upon the concerns and priorities that Scripture already presents, allowing God's Word to serve as both the foundation and the framework for our moral worldview and preparing us to answer the ethical questions we do not yet even know to ask."

—**Katie J. McCoy**, director of women's ministry, Baptist General Convention of Texas

"In this most welcome series on Christian ethics, Jacob Shatzer hits the bull's-eye with an excellent primer on biblical ethics. This work is informed by recent scholarship, normed by the story of the Bible, relevant for the challenges of today, and practical for all Christians. Shatzer carefully avoids the 'strip-mining approach' to biblical ethics that simply throws a few verses at complicated moral issues. Instead, he teaches us how to be handled by the Scripture—and not the other way around—while being oriented toward a lifetime of careful obedience to Christ by the reading and rereading of his Word."

—**Benjamin Quinn**, associate professor of theology and history of ideas, Southeastern Baptist Theological Seminary

BIBLICAL ETHICS

ESSENTIALS *in Christian Ethics*

BIBLICAL ETHICS

A Short Companion

Jacob Shatzer

editors
C. Ben Mitchell & Jason Thacker

ACADEMIC
BRENTWOOD, TENNESSEE

Biblical Ethics: A Short Companion

Published by B&H Academic
Brentwood, Tennessee

ISBN: 978-1-0877-7544-9

Dewey Decimal Classification: 241
Subject Heading: CHRISTIAN ETHICS \ ETHICS \ BIBLE--ETHICS

Cover design by Emily Keafer Lambright. Cover illustration by J614/iStock.

Printed in the United States of America

29 28 27 26 25 24 VP 1 2 3 4 5 6 7 8 9 10

For Ezekiel, as the Lord awakens in you
a joy for studying his Word

Christian reading and interpreting of the Bible is an instance of itself. The complex configuration of text-acts and reading-acts, the use of this text with those intentions to achieve these ends, is sui generis. *It is not, of course, wholly dissimilar from other acts of reading undertaken by other readers in other communities with other purposes and self-definitions. But establishing the commonplaces and overlaps between Christian and other acts of reading, however valuable in exposing docetism, often serves the purpose of underwriting a foundational anthropology which eclipses what in fact is most interesting about what happens when Christians read the Bible: that the Bible as text is the* viva vox Dei *addressing the people of God and generating faith and obedience. It is this address which is constitutive of the Christian hermeneutical situation, and it is this which in the last analysis means that that situation is without analogies.*

—John Webster, *Word and Church*

CONTENTS

Series Preface by C. Ben Mitchell and Jason Thacker xiii

Chapter 1 What Is Biblical Ethics? 1
Chapter 2 The Overarching Story 27
Chapter 3 Covenants and Redemption 51
Chapter 4 Old and New Testament Ethics 67
Chapter 5 A Whole-Bible Biblical Ethics 95
Chapter 6 Challenges to Biblical Ethics 107
Chapter 7 The Practice of Biblical Ethics 135

For Further Reading 149
Acknowledgments 151
Subject Index 153

SERIES PREFACE

In 1876, German Lutheran theologian Christoph Ernst Luthardt eloquently illustrated the relationship between theology and ethics. He wrote, "God first loved us is the summary of Christian doctrine. We love Him is the summary of Christian morality."[1] The wedding of theology and ethics was later embraced by generations of theologians and ethicists, such as Protestant titans Herman Bavinck and Carl F. H. Henry,[2] who rightly understood the primacy of both theology and ethics in the Christian life. But at times in the recent history of the Protestant church, the study of ethics has been relegated to a mere application of theology and biblical studies rather than understood as a first-order discipline in rich partnership with the theological task.

The aim of the Christian ethic can be summed up in the words of Jesus in Matt 22:37–39. We, God's people, are to "love the Lord

---

[1] Christoph Ernst Luthardt, *Apologetic Lectures on the Moral Truths of Christianity*, trans. Sophia Taylor (Edinburgh: T&T Clark, 1876), 26.

[2] See Herman Bavinck, *Reformed Ethics*. ed. John Bolt, vol. 1, *Created, Fallen, and Converted Humanity* (Grand Rapids: Baker, 2019), §1:58; and Carl F. H. Henry, *Christian Personal Ethics*, 2nd ed. (Grand Rapids: Baker, 1979), 486.

[our] God with all [our] heart[s] and with all [our] soul[s] and with all [our] mind[s] . . . and to love [our] neighbor as [ourselves]." We hear echoes of this summation in the words of Luthardt, Bavinck, and Henry, each of whom spoke of how God's people are to love him as the summary of Christian morality. Thus, Christian ethics is nothing less than a primary motivation for those seeking to be faithful to God in all of life and live in light of how he has revealed himself in Scripture. Ethics as discipleship is a key theme throughout Scripture and one the church must elevate as we seek God's face in the academy, in our churches, and especially in our personal lives as transformed creatures made in the very image of God.

While Christian ethics is a core element of God's revelation to his people about how they are to live as his followers, it is also a distinct philosophical discipline that must be studied in consideration of the rich history of moral thought seen throughout the life of the church and the wider society. Much of today's discourse about Christian ethics tends to focus on the mere application of theological or philosophical principles, rather than on understanding how these principles have been derived and refined over time in light of the massive metaphysical and epistemological shifts in the history of thought.

Given the recent tendency in wider evangelicalism at times to downplay the direct study of ethics in our curricula, in our church life, and in the task of discipleship, the Essentials in Christian Ethics series is designed to illuminate the richness of the Christian ethic, as well as how ethics is intricately woven into the whole of the Christian life. We have gathered renowned ethicists and leading figures in their fields of theological and philosophical inquiry who are passionate about proclaiming the biblical ethic to a world desperately in need of Christ.

The series is made up of short, introductory volumes spanning metaethics, normative ethics, and applied ethics. Each volume can be used independently as an introduction to the crucial elements of the Christian ethical tradition, including resources for further reading and key concepts for those seeking to dig deeper into the beauty of God's revelation. They can also be used as supplements to a larger ethics curriculum, where a specialized volume could be used to augment a primary text or to give deeper insight into particular contemporary ethical debates.

As editors, we have longed for a series like this to be written by scholars who understand and apply the rich relationship of theology and ethics in their teaching, writings, and ministry. This series is designed to model for readers how the biblical ethic applies to every area of life both as a distinct theological and a philosophical discipline in the context of the Christian moral tradition from a robust Protestant viewpoint. We pray this serves the wider academy, those training in our colleges and seminaries, and especially those seeking to employ the riches of Christian ethics in the context of the local church.

C. Ben Mitchell and Jason Thacker
Series Editors

1

What Is Biblical Ethics?

I do not mean to alarm you, but the word *natural* is often used when marketing products that may or may not be so "natural." In fact, the US Food and Drug Administration has requested comments from the public on the use of this label in human food products because there is so much confusion about it.[1] Many companies have seen that labeling a product "natural" can increase its sales, and since there is no clear regulated definition of the term, its use has increased.

Consider another term: *biblical*. It is quite the claim to stick "biblical" on the front of something. Biblical preaching. Biblical theology. Biblical counseling. The term "biblical" can function in multiple ways. At the most basic level, "biblical" might mean something like "as approved by the Bible" or "as taught by the Bible."

[1] "Use of the Term Natural on Food Labeling," FDA website, accessed February 15, 2023, https://www.fda.gov/food/food-labeling-nutrition/use-term-natural-food-labeling.

For some, "biblical" simply means "right." While "biblical" can serve in this basic descriptive way, terms often change and take on additional meaning. In fact, "biblical preaching" is a sort of preaching that some set over against other types of preaching, some of which might also involve the Bible. The same occurs with "biblical theology." This term has come to mean not simply "any theology that corresponds to what the Bible teaches," but instead a particular approach to putting theology together, understanding theology, articulating theology, and applying theology. In recent years "biblical counseling" has also developed a particular definition, one that means not simply "counseling done by someone who occasionally uses Bible verses" but instead a particular set of methodological commitments and processes for counseling, set over against other approaches with different commitments.

Due to this confusion, some shake their heads at the notion of "biblical" anything, skeptically placing the term itself in scare quotes.

We do not need to go that far. We simply need to be aware that describing something as "biblical" raises the question of what exactly that adjective is doing. What does it mean for someone to claim to be a biblical preacher or to be writing biblical theology? Or, for the task before us now: What does it mean to claim "biblical ethics"?

Samples of Answers

I do not claim to have the only answer to this question. Let's look at just a few possibilities, some from daily life and others from scholarship.[2]

---

[2] For a treatment of several theologians from the twentieth century and how they used Scripture for ethics, see Jeffrey S. Siker, *Scripture and Ethics: Twentieth-Century Portraits* (New York: Oxford, 1997).

First, biblical ethics can simply mean "right." Some people use the term "biblical ethics" to mean an ethical position or system of ethical positions that they view to be consistent with the Bible. You have likely heard this statement in a church setting or perhaps seen it in a stream of comments on social media. Used this way, the term tells us more about what the speaker thinks about the ethical position than it does about how the idea is truly *biblical.* In this case, "biblical" serves as a blanket approval.

Second, biblical ethics can mean ethics with chapter and verse. We sometimes use "biblical ethics" in another plain and basic sense, something close to simple "proof texting." In this approach, an ethical position is called biblical if it is explained using Bible verses. It might be one of the Ten Commandments, or something from Jesus, as long as it seems to support whatever ethical claim is being made. For example, "Do not commit adultery" (Exod 20:14). Pretty clear and straightforward! Statement (verse reference) = biblical ethics. This way of using the term gives more information than the previous one—since it enables you to look at a specific verse or passage—but it still leaves the connection between the Bible and the ethical position unarticulated. In many cases, it is that simple; but why? And we lose something when we leave the "why" out.

Third, biblical ethics can take some portion of the Bible and describe its ethical position. While the first two tend to focus on individual issues and declare which positions are correct, this third approach to biblical ethics starts with the text itself, seeking to see ethics from its context-driven viewpoint, and then to apply

---

Further, Craig Bartholomew provides five answers to how the Bible has been used ethically. See his introduction in *A Royal Priesthood?: The Use of the Bible Ethically and Politically*, ed. Craig Bartholomew et al. (Grand Rapids: Zondervan, 2002), 12–19.

that viewpoint toward contemporary situations. For example, Christopher J. H. Wright and Richard B. Hays have produced volumes focused on Old Testament ethics and New Testament ethics, respectively. Wright emphasizes that Old Testament ethics is built upon Israel's worldview and that we have to put ourselves in their position to understand how their experiences with God impacted the way they thought about ethics and lived as a community.[3] Hays seeks to hear each individual voice that speaks on ethical issues, and he pursues a common theme where possible.[4] Hays's approach to biblical ethics gives a clearer voice to the Bible itself, but sometimes broader biblical connections are left unexplored or the overall narrative of the Bible is downplayed. For example, Hays's nearly 500-page book includes only three pages explicitly addressing the role of the Old Testament in New Testament ethics. While this may be understandable with as much material as Hays does cover, it is still an obvious limitation of a focus on New Testament ethics. Some scholars go even further, arguing that biblical ethics, because it is only about the Bible and its time, is insufficient for a contemporary Christian ethics.[5]

Fourth, biblical ethics might mean the Bible is the ultimate authority and dictates the method of ethics. In other words, some define biblical ethics based on its approach to authority and ethical method. For instance, David Jones explains, "Biblical ethics

---

[3] See Christopher J. H. Wright, *Old Testament Ethics for the People of God* (Downers Grove, IL: IVP Academic, 2004), 17.

[4] See Richard B. Hays, *The Moral Vision of the New Testament: A Contemporary Introduction to New Testament Ethics* (San Francisco: HarperOne, 1996), 15.

[5] See Bruce C. Birch and Larry L. Rasmussen, *Bible and Ethics in the Christian Life*, rev. and exp. ed. (Minneapolis: Augsburg, 1989), 12. We will discuss approaches like this one later in the book.

differs from secular ethics . . . in that it is distinctively Christian in its approach to ethical evaluation as it uses the Bible as its source of moral authority."[6] Further, it "is more specific than Christian ethics proper in that it specifically focuses on the study, structure, and application of the moral law as it is revealed in Scripture."[7] For Jones, this approach leads him to focus on ethics refracted through the Ten Commandments. In Robertson McQuilkin and Paul Copan's *An Introduction to Biblical Ethics*, the authors root their understanding of biblical ethics in living wisely in relation to what God has revealed in the Bible. This thinking presses them to consider love, law, sin, virtues, and vices and then to apply the Bible to specific issues.[8]

Fifth, biblical ethics might just mean ethics connected to a Christian theistic worldview. Some scholars, such as Allen Verhey, use "biblical ethics" in a broad, general sense. Verhey says that biblical ethics is "inalienably theological," and he explains its fundamental unity as "there is one God in Scripture, and it is that one God who calls forth the creative reflection and faithful response of those who would be God's people." Yet, "the one God of Scripture assures the unity of biblical ethics, but there is no simple unitive understanding even of that one God or of that one God's will."[9]

Clearly, we will need to clarify what we mean by biblical ethics. Let's begin with a quick refresher on ethics itself.

---

[6] David W. Jones, *An Introduction to Biblical Ethics* (Nashville: B&H Academic, 2013), 2.

[7] Jones, 2.

[8] See Robertson McQuilkin and Paul Copan, *An Introduction to Biblical Ethics: Walking in the Way of Wisdom*, 3rd ed. (Downers Grove, IL: IVP Academic, 2014).

[9] Allen Verhey, "Ethics in Scripture," in *Dictionary of Scripture and Ethics*, ed. Joel B. Green (Grand Rapids: Baker, 2011), 5.

The Task of Ethics

Let's zoom out to the bigger picture for a moment and ensure that we understand what ethics is. In his article entitled "Ethics in Scripture," Allen Verhey defines ethics "as disciplined reflection concerning moral conduct and character."[10] Scott Rae, author of one of the most popular evangelical ethics textbooks, provides some helpful definitions. While many people switch between "morality" and "ethics" without much distinction, strictly speaking, "morality refers to the actual *content* of right and wrong, and ethics refers to the *process* of determining, or discovering, right and wrong. In other words, morality deals with moral *knowledge* and ethics with moral *reasoning and justification*."[11] Ethics is concerned with knowing and doing what is right. In particular, the task of ethics is on articulating and undertaking a process for pursuing the moral life.

Knowing right and wrong might seem fairly intuitive in some cases, but this task is more challenging than you might think. As one author puts it, "Where do most people get their ethical beliefs, their judgments about right and wrong? For most modern Westerners—that is, those of us who live in the post-Enlightenment global West—our moral beliefs come from a complex combination of everything that makes up one's context."[12] In other words, we do not get our ethical beliefs in a systematic way, organized around a primary authority. Instead, we simply pick them up as we go along, from a variety of sources, including family, church, popular culture and media, school, and so on. We do not always reflect carefully on

---

[10] Allen Verhey, "Ethics in Scripture," 5.

[11] Scott B. Rae, *Moral Choices: An Introduction to Ethics*, 4th ed. (Grand Rapids: Zondervan Academic, 2018), 19–20 (emphasis original).

[12] Keith Stanglin, *Ethics Beyond Rules: How Christ's Call to Love Informs Our Moral Choices* (Grand Rapids: Zondervan, 2021), xv.

the nature of the authorities we try to blend together in our own understandings of right and wrong.

When we consider biblical ethics, then, we are talking about a process for coming to know and do the right actions. At the same time, biblical ethics recognizes that these actions are always done by people, dependent on their character and their circumstances, including their membership within a particular people (in the case of the Bible, the people of God).

Biblical ethics, the process of discerning right and wrong rooted in and in response to Scripture, obviously depends to a great degree on what exactly the Bible is and how it directs our thinking and doing.

The Bible

Before we begin to build out exactly what biblical ethics might look like, we need to focus some attention on what the Bible is and how it means. (Yes, *how* it means, as in how the Bible communicates meaning and becomes meaning-*full*.) Statements about the Bible's authority—its status as God's inerrant Word, rooted in the truthful character of our graciously communicative God—are fundamental and necessary in understanding the authority of biblical ethics. If we do not understand how the Bible develops meaning, our biblical ethics will remain flat.

The Bible communicates truth in many ways. For instance, we all recognize that the Bible contains stories, which teach us truths about God in ways that are different from, say, a doctrine textbook. The Bible's use of stories does not mean it is not true; stories, after all, can be true. Similarly, we are usually good at identifying when the Bible uses poetry. This is not because we are all experts in poetry—and certainly not Hebrew poetry—but because we know that poetry *looks* a certain way on the printed page. The same idea about truth applies: the Bible's stories are true, and the Bible's poetry is true.

We all know that stories and poetry work in different ways, ways different from one another and from other types of writing. If we are going to understand the stories and poems correctly, we should take these differences into account as we read and seek to understand. Stories and poetry are not the only two types of writing God uses in the Bible. While Scripture communicates clearly—what theologians refer to as the "perspicuity" of Scripture—we still have to think about the way God speaks truth in the Bible.[13] Stories and poetry work a bit differently, as we have noted.

Beyond the difference in genres of literature, we also should understand the way the Bible uses symbols to tell its stories and to tie its stories together into one Big Story. Just as stories and poetry do not mean that the material is not true, so also the Bible's use of symbols does not mean that its stories are made up. Christians who have a high view of Scripture—seeing it as the inerrant Word of a good God seeking to reconcile his people to himself—can still recognize and understand the way God uses symbols to make these connections across these true stories to bring together his Story. In short, symbols do not mean a story is false or fabricated.

As biblical scholars and theologians have paid more attention to the way the Bible communicates truth across the entire canon, the discipline of biblical theology has become more significant. Biblical theology provides a more helpful framework for a healthy and robust biblical ethics because it helps us avoid

[13] For more on the Bible's authority, see D. A. Carson, ed., *The Enduring Authority of the Christian Scriptures* (Grand Rapids: Eerdmans, 2016).

segmenting the text and instead aids us in responding to its overall narrative and force. Understanding the work of biblical theology will pay dividends as we seek to hear and obey the unified voice of God in Scripture.

Biblical theology attempts to draw together the entire canon (or major sections of the canon) to understand what the Bible progressively reveals about specific topics.[14] Brian Rosner defines biblical theology as "theological interpretation of Scripture in and for the church. It proceeds with historical and literary sensitivity and seeks to analyze and synthesize the Bible's teaching about God and his relations to the world on its own terms, maintaining the sight of the Bible's overarching narrative and Christocentric focus."[15] So, while some practices of theology might layer more abstract concepts "on top" of the Bible, biblical theology attempts to use the interpretive perspective of the biblical authors to understand what God progressively reveals about himself.

James Hamilton has provided a helpful introduction to this field in his book *What Is Biblical Theology? A Guide to the Bible's Story, Symbolism, and Patterns*. He defines biblical theology as an interpretive perspective that the biblical authors held and that we find reflected in the way they present their understanding of other writings in the Bible.[16] Biblical theologians attempt to think in categories familiar to biblical authors while also tracing the way

---

[14] See Peter J. Gentry and Stephen J. Wellum, *Kingdom through Covenant: A Biblical-Theological Understanding of the Covenants*, 2nd ed. (Wheaton, IL: Crossway, 2018), 39.

[15] Brian Rosner, "Biblical Theology," in *New Dictionary of Biblical Theology*, ed. T. Desmond Alexander et al. (Downers Grove, IL: Intervarsity Press, 2000), 10.

[16] James M. Hamilton Jr., *What Is Biblical Theology?: A Guide to the Bible's Story, Symbolism, and Patterns* (Wheaton, IL: Crossway, 2013), 16.

God progressively reveals truth through different writers in different books at different times.

This practice is important because if we only carry our modern assumptions to the text, we will miss much of what God has to say to us there. But if we allow the Bible's narrative, symbols, and framework to set the stage, we will be better equipped to understand what the Bible might have to say about ethics, rather than allowing our own assumptions to drive our interpretation. We must remember that the Bible only makes sense when understood within God's actions of redemption. As John Webster puts it, "Scripture and therefore the canon are ordered towards this economy; they are elements in a dynamic and purposive field of relations between the triune God and his creatures."[17] Hamilton's work will guide us as we seek to grasp the basics of what he calls the Bible's "symbolic universe." The symbolic universe requires us to think about symbols, imagery, typology, and patterns.

Symbols

Symbols stand for something. Sports teams have symbols. Political parties have symbols. These symbols mean more to us than the literal depiction of the symbol.[18] For instance, I'm a Cubs fan. The Cubs "symbol" or logo calls to mind all sorts of things for me—my late grandfather's collection of Cubs memorabilia, trips with him to see games at Wrigley Field, and a photo I have in my office of me holding my four (young) children at the conclusion of the Cubs' 2016 seventh-game World Series victory. It's more than just a red letter *C* or a small bear. The same applies for other symbols. It is how they work.

---

[17] John Webster, *Word and Church* (New York: T&T Clark, 2016), 28.

[18] See Hamilton, *What Is Biblical Theology?*, 65.

We often use symbols in our communication, and understanding communication often requires understanding the associations between the symbols used.

The biblical writers developed symbolism by using and repeating different images.[19] As we might expect, recognizing and understanding these images is vital to getting the story.[20] Hamilton uses Leviticus as an example because Moses doesn't take the time to explain the different symbolic acts in play in the sacrificial system. Everyone in his original audience understood these symbols; they had seen blood sacrifice. Most of us, thousands of years later, haven't. To understand the Bible's symbols in Leviticus, we have to try more carefully to understand.[21]

In other words, if we want to understand what the original authors were trying to communicate, we must attempt to grasp the symbols and other elements that they would have taken for granted, assuming their audience would understand. We are often good about thinking through cultural items we might not understand ("How much is a denarius, anyway?"), but this also applies to symbols and images that carry through the Bible.

Authors use the elements making up the symbolic universe of the text that combine and work together to convey meaning. As stated earlier, this emphasis on symbols, images, and patterns does not mean the events of the text did not happen. The God who is sovereign over history is also author of the text, so the actual occurrence of the symbolic elements of the stories does not take away from their symbolic value. In other words, looking for images, types, and patterns does not mean downplaying the historical value

---

[19] See Hamilton, 62.

[20] See Hamilton, 63.

[21] See Hamilton, 64.

of the text. Instead, this approach recognizes that the God of history is also the God inspiring the text. He is the one guiding the symbolic universe as these elements interact to create and convey meaning together. Layering symbols creates "texture" in the Bible's story, and these symbols reinforce the story and make it increasingly real to readers.[22] Thus, understanding this symbolic universe is not optional.

Now that we have emphasized the importance of symbolism, we need to understand better what elements make it work. We will turn next to imagery.

Images

The Bible uses images to illustrate complicated ideas and to connect different concepts in the broader story. The authors of the Bible recognize the complexity of ideas, and they reach for symbols to help their audience get it.[23] The images, then, serve both to explain and to connect.

One example of this can be seen in the image of the flood works in the Bible's story.[24] There are numerous parallels between the flood and the creation story, showing correspondences between Adam and Noah. For instance, God parts the waters to make dry land appear (Gen 1:9–10), while the flood covers that dry land back up. Further, "as Adam sinned by eating of the tree in Genesis 3, Noah also sinned by abusing the fruit of the vine in Genesis 9. In both cases, nakedness was exposed then covered.

[22] See Hamilton, 65.

[23] See Hamilton, 67.

[24] For Hamilton's development of this, see 70–72.

God's judgment was visited in the waters of the flood, but the flood did not wash away human sin."[25] The flood's imagery does not end there.

Later points in the Bible's story pick up this imagery as well. Moses uses the same term to describe Noah's ark and the basket into which Moses's mother put him in Exod 2:3: both Noah and Moses were saved through the waters in an "ark."[26] Later biblical writers use the flood imagery to point to God's judgment, including armies described as a flood (Psalm 125 and Isaiah 8), and both Jesus and Peter in the New Testament use flood imagery in their discussions of baptism (Mark 10:38–39; 1 Pet 3:20–21). The flood connects to the Bible's storyline in many ways—sin and judgment, salvation, the waters of God's wrath that are poured out on Israel's enemies and on sin at the cross. In short, "just as Noah was saved through the visitation of God's wrath on the world, those who believe in Jesus are saved through the visitation of God's wrath at the cross."[27]

The communication of the gospel, in other words, takes up images established in the flood. Ignoring these images impoverishes our understanding because they are images not merely created by a human author, or added by a human editor, but inspired throughout the entire Bible text with its various human authors by its one divine Author.

If we do not pick up these images and symbols, we miss out on part of the story. They serve an important role because they summarize the story and provide further interpretation.[28]

---

[25] Hamilton, 70.

[26] Hamilton, 70.

[27] Hamilton, 71–72.

[28] Hamilton, 75.

Typology

Typology is a literary device that uses and connects images and ideas in important ways. At its most basic, typology includes one or more "types" and an eventual "antitype." The types point toward and prepare us for the antitype—the fulfillment, the end for which the types prepare us and to which they point. The types, then, are significant not only in what we learn about them but in how they teach us and help us to understand later antitypes. The biggest example of this is the variety of Old Testament figures who point forward to Christ in various ways. Jesus then fulfills not only the law but also these types.

We must define typology carefully, especially in order to avoid allegory. Allegory finds parallels between the text and today, but those parallels are often driven by hidden symbolism or quick assumptions, rather than being driven by the text, historically understood. Peter Gentry and Stephen Wellum give a helpful treatment of typology in their *Kingdom through Covenants*. First, they note that typology is rooted in both the history and the text of the Bible.[29] Second, they argue that typology is intended by God; it is prophetic and predictive. In fact, considering typology as a type of prophecy is a key move not only in connecting it properly within the text but also in avoiding abuses of modern distortion. Gentry and Wellum also highlight three basic characteristics of typology. First, it involves a repetition of a person, event, or institution, but ultimately these types are fulfilled in Christ and then in the church.[30] In other words, biblical typology is Christological and ecclesiological. The connections are fulfilled in Christ. Gentry and

---

[29] Gentry and Wellum, *Kingdom through Covenant*, 130.

[30] Gentry and Wellum, 131.

Wellum's second characteristic is that the types move from lesser to greater, but not necessarily in a progression. There might be three or four types that form a link to Christ. Christ is indeed greater, but type 3 might not be greater than type 2. For example, drawing a typological link from Adam to David to Christ certainly places Christ as the greater type, but does not necessarily imply anything about the relationship between Adam and David. Gentry and Wellum highlight one more characteristic: types develop through the progression of covenants in the Bible.[31] This is one of the reasons we will deal with covenants in a later chapter.

We can boil this down to two important features in the Bible's use of typology. First, *historical correspondence* matches up real people with events. Second, *escalation* explains how we move through the pattern of correspondence, which gathers momentum until the final fulfillment is revealed.[32] This notion of historical context and escalation helps us see how types are related but also different from one another.

As mentioned earlier, looking for a literary device such as typology does not mean it is *only* a literary device. Characters in a made-up story can be typologically related, but noticing typology does not imply that the Bible is mere narrative. In reality, when we identify typological connections, we see the sovereignty of God working in history to connect real people, events, and institutions in meaningful ways.[33]

Typology can connect people. Hamilton uses the example of Moses and Jesus. Pharaoh tried to kill baby Moses; Herod attempted the same with the baby Jesus. Moses and Jesus and their

---

[31] See Gentry and Wellum, 135.

[32] See Hamilton, *What Is Biblical Theology?*, 77.

[33] See Hamilton, 78.

parents were strangers in Egypt. Moses led the people of God in the wilderness, where they were tempted and eventually gave in to sin. Jesus went into the wilderness and, though tempted, did not sin. Moses went up on a mountain, Mount Sinai, to get a law from God. Jesus went up on a mountain where he sat down and taught his law, the Sermon on the Mount. Escalation occurs between Moses and Jesus. Moses led Israel out of slavery, and Jesus saves his people from slavery too—slavery to sin. Moses led God's people into a Promised Land that was a shadow of a new "Eden," and Jesus will lead his people into the ultimate New Eden—the new heaven and earth.[34] Thus, to understand Jesus and his work, it helps to understand the way God used Moses too.

Typology can also connect events. Continuing with Hamilton's examples, we can see parallels between the event of the exodus and Jesus's work. To look at only one small part, God brought a people out of slavery, gave them a covenant, and had them build a tabernacle. Jesus brings people out of slavery to sin, gives the new covenant, and builds his people into a spiritual temple.

Finally, typology can connect institutions. We see this typology explicitly in the book of Hebrews. The priesthood and the sacrificial system point to and give way to something far superior in the ministry of Christ (Hebrews 10). The author of the book of Hebrews demonstrates throughout the book that Jesus is superior to previous institutions: the priesthood, the sacrificial system, Moses, the angels, and more. The author is not trying to say that those previous things do not matter. Rather, he is drawing out the archetype-fulfillment pattern to show that as great as those previous institutions were in God's plan, part of what they were doing was pointing forward to the greater and final ministry of Jesus

---

[34] See Hamilton, 79.

Christ. Here we see how typology serves not only to connect different parts of the story but also to help us see the supremacy of Christ. The escalation element of typology reminds us that as great as previous types are, they build to demonstrate the supremacy of the ultimate fulfillment. In other words, the New Testament writers are not merely helping us see connections in God's plan; they are using those connections to argue for the all-surpassing greatness of Christ.

One last way of considering the Bible's symbolic universe is to consider other patterns that are present in the text.

Patterns

We all recognize patterns, and we even see patterns in the Bible without necessarily giving them much thought. Patterns do something, however; they teach us about reality and the way things are supposed to be. Patterns teach us that there is something that normally happens, and thus we learn to notice it and to expect it.[35] In other words, when we see patterns, we are learning something about how God works and what we might expect from him in the future. Clearly, patterns do not limit God's freedom, but they serve as a device for him to reveal his way of working and to provide hope for the future. Patterns also help us see how the entire Bible story fits together in ways that make sense.

Not only do these patterns ultimately point to Christ and find its fulfillment in him; they also set up for his followers what we are to expect in this world. God gives us the symbols so that they will shape the way we understand ourselves and the story we are in fact

---

[35] See Hamilton, 87.

in.[36] Just as Jesus fulfills the pattern of the righteous sufferer, we like Paul should experience our sufferings as privileges to be connected to Christ (e.g., Col 1:24–2:15). These symbols, whether images or types or patterns, draw us in and help us make sense of our lives.[37] If we do not recognize this symbolic universe, we will miss some of what God is revealing to us in the Bible's story.

The Bible's symbolic universe is not necessarily obvious on a first reading. We need the habits of careful readers to notice the way these symbols, images, types, and patterns fit together, and we need to read a lot of the Bible repeatedly to pick them up. However, because God uses these devices to reveal his truth, it is important that we look for them and are open to learning from others who have identified patterns. Later in the book, we will consider some ways that the Bible's symbolic universe communicates truth to us about our expectations of ethics.

Biblical Ethics at the Intersection

When we consider the task of ethics and the nature of Scripture, what biblical ethics must be emerges into view. Biblical ethics cannot merely be the citing of a verse or two, or a trite label for our own opinions. Instead, biblical ethics must approach the task of ethics according to the nature of Scripture. Biblical ethics provides for the progressive and unfolding nature of God's Word to create a matrix of commands, values, and virtues embedded in an ongoing story, a story in which we still find ourselves and our ethical challenges. Biblical ethics is not something we accomplish by aligning our ethical thinking with some preconceived position. Biblical

[36] See Hamilton, 90.

[37] See Hamilton, 90.

ethics is not really a methodology for starting with an issue and searching out key texts (though this can occur once the groundwork has been properly laid). Instead, biblical ethics is a commitment to immersion in the biblical text and to undergoing its formative power before, during, and after our consideration of particular ethical challenges. Biblical ethics reads with the grain of Scripture,[38] emerging from the world of the biblical text for faithful living in the present rather than occasionally diving into the Bible to extract "answers." In brief, biblical ethics seeks to emerge out of the warp and woof, the fabric, of the world of the Bible and God's promises and work to understand where we are and what faithful living looks like here and now.

Biblical ethics does not only stand at the intersection of the task of ethics and the nature of Scripture. It also draws on several other conversations, including the nature and function of law in the Bible and the different ethical systems proposed by ethicists. We will touch on each of these briefly here.

The Christian and the Law

Since biblical ethics requires understanding how the Bible fits together and drives toward right thought and action, the overlap between this discussion and the Christian understanding of the gospel and the law should be obvious. Biblical ethics lines up closely with the question, "How does the Christian relate to the Old Testament law?" Thomas Schreiner helpfully notes, "In both the Old and New Testaments, the word *law* focuses on the commands and regulations of the Mosaic covenant. In most instances

[38] I'm drawing this language specifically from Richard B. Hays, *Reading with the Grain of Scripture* (Grand Rapids: Eerdmans, 2020).

the word *law* does not refer to instruction in a general sense but concentrates on what God demands that his people do."[39] When we enter this territory, however, we must realize that, as one scholar puts it, "There is no consensus of understanding of the relationship between Law and Gospel."[40] I will not pretend to solve this issue here, but I will argue that there is an underlying unity in the Bible's treatment of law and gospel that also lends unity to biblical ethics. Engaging this discussion can help us better understand the unity of the Bible and its ethical commitments and demands.

Drawing from the work of John Calvin,[41] Protestant Christians have highlighted three different uses of the law, and those uses take their logic from the place within the biblical story that we find the law and that we find ourselves. First, the law is an instrument of righteousness that convicts us and warns us of our unrighteousness. Second, the law works as a moral teacher, instructing sinful people about the will of good and right action. Third and finally, the law restrains sinners from sinning as much as we might and doing as much harm as we otherwise would.[42] Though this position is embraced most clearly in a Reformed articulation of law and gospel, these basic uses fit various interpretations of this issue.

The key issue revolves around the law's purpose at any individual point in Scripture, how that purpose fits with the part of

---

[39] Thomas R. Schreiner, *40 Questions about Christians and Biblical Law* (Grand Rapids: Kregel, 2010), 23.

[40] Wayne G. Strickland, "Preface," in *Five Views on Law and Gospel*, ed. Wayne G. Strickland (Grand Rapids: Zondervan, 1996), 9.

[41] See John Calvin, *Institutes of the Christian Religion* 2.7.6–12.

[42] See Willem VanGemeren, "The Law Is the Perfection of Righteousness in Jesus Christ: A Reformed Perspective," in Strickland, *Five Views on Law and Gospel*, 53.

the narrative in which the law is found and applied, and what happens to those laws as the narrative moves along. Christians agree that one purpose of the law is to show people the character of God. For some, this means that all laws continue to be binding on everyone because the character of God does not change.[43] Unless a law is explicitly canceled, it remains in force. For others, the individual laws demonstrate God's eternal character, yes, but in a way appropriate to and bound by the particular stage of God's redemptive plan.[44] Additionally, the purpose of the law is not only to align God's people with God's character, but to communicate God's character to a watching world (as a "light to the nations"). Not only that, but Christ's role in fulfilling the law and inaugurating a new covenant significantly shapes the way we understand the laws in the Old Testament and how they apply today as the church seeks to bear witness in word and in deed to the kingdom of God.

If God's character and action and revelation and salvation are consistent and unified, it follows that by the help of the Holy Spirit we can hear God's unified voice calling us to holiness, consistently, through the Bible. But listening for this voice requires us to understand the Old Testament narrative, the New Testament narrative, and the unified biblical narrative in a way that helps us make sense of God's ethical vision, commands, and values at any point. In upcoming chapters, we will explore these narratives in more depth to better understand the unity of biblical ethics.

---

[43] For example, see Greg Bahnsen, "The Law, the Gospel, and the Modern Christian," in Strickland, *Five Views on Law and Gospel*, 93–143.

[44] For instance, see Douglas Moo, "The Law of Christ and the Fulfillment of the Law of Moses," in Strickland, *Five Views on Law and Gospel*, 319–76.

Ethical Systems

When we attempt to understand biblical ethics and to actually *do* biblical ethics, we find ourselves at another intersection: different types of moral reasoning. We encounter all sorts of systems for moral reasoning in our day-to-day lives, some consistent, some not. How does biblical ethics, as we are exploring it in this chapter, fit within that landscape?

Returning again to *Moral Choices*, we see that Scott Rae highlights several types of moral reasoning we might encounter.[45] We would stray too far afield to explore each of these systems in depth—and any attempt to introduce briefly will necessarily simplify—but a quick overview will help us recognize how biblical ethics might survive (and even thrive) in the intersection of this perennial debate.[46] One group of these approaches does not fit with any sense of biblical ethics, while another group of approaches can find some affinity. But even those that do not seem to fit betray themselves, indicating something about ethics that the Bible anticipates, as we will see.

Several types of moral reasoning simply fail to account for any sense of biblical authority at all and are thus difficult to connect to biblical ethics. Emotivism, for instance, holds that moral judgments are simply ways for us to express our emotions about a particular topic or issue. Utilitarianisms find morality solely in an action's result. Ethical egoism roots morality primarily in self-interest.

---

[45] For this discussion in more detail, see Rae, *Moral Choices*, 38–65.

[46] For an in-depth treatment of contemporary Christian views, see Steve Wilkens, ed., *Christian Ethics: Four Views* (Downers Grove, IL: IVP Academic, 2017).

Ethical relativism argues that right and wrong emerge from particular cultural decisions and expressions, without any universal applicability. These systems leave little room for an authority of any sort outside the self or culture.

At the same time, these systems indicate something about what humans look for and long for when we encounter ethical issues. While these systems do not make room for an authoritative Bible, a biblical ethics can acknowledge and address some of these root issues. For instance, ethics has often cut the heart out of difficult situations, leaving emotions out, which emotivism seeks to correct—and overcorrects. Further, humans expect right choices to lead to good consequences, most of the time. Utilitarianisms, which vary in their methods, take that sentiment and run it backward, from the results to the actions in order to justify what counts as "good." A misstep, to be sure, but the Bible does in fact recognize the connection between right action and right consequences (but it also recognizes that such correspondence is not always the case).

Other types of moral reasoning fit more consistently with biblical ethics. Deontological ethics bases right and wrong on unchanging principles and values. Rules and commands fit here, though some scholars separate out a divine command ethics, which works similarly but roots the principles and values entirely in God's will and command, not in philosophical reasoning. Virtue ethics, on the other hand, focuses on more than doing the right thing; instead, ethics is about the type of person you are becoming. Both of these systems fit more readily with the Bible as an authoritative text, giving either rules or the types of virtues that Christians should seek.

One more system has an awkward fit: natural law.[47] As one scholar explains, "Natural law theory believes that moral precepts exist independently of our judgments, are binding on all people, and are knowable by reason."[48] You can see why this view fits awkwardly. While natural law can fit alongside an ethic that derives significant direction from the Bible, its insistence on the knowability of morality by reason alone makes the Bible at least somewhat unnecessary. It has seen popularity throughout church history, however, given the metaphysical realities of God's creation of humanity and a moral universe. Charles Cosgrove argues that "on many topics the church fathers worked out views consistent with the ethics of Greek and Roman philosophers by claiming that the Greeks had stolen their ideas from Moses and by articulating a theory of natural law available to all human beings."[49] Stolen from Moses or not, these ideas have deeply shaped Christian thinking on ethics.

We often experience these types of moral reasoning as competitors. Is morality determined by culture (moral relativism)? Is it determined and communicated by God (divine command theory)? Do we have to figure it out ourselves, either through reason (deontology), the world around us (natural law), by analyzing consequences (utilitarianism), or simply by stating our own preferences and good (emotivism or ethical egoism)? Even narrowing the debate to Christians, "divine command theory, virtue ethics,

---

[47] See David VanDrunen, *Natural Law: A Short Companion*, ed. C. Ben Mitchell and Jason Thacker (Brentwood, TN: B&H Academic, 2023).

[48] Steve Wilkens, "Introduction to Four Theories of *Christian* Ethics," in *Christian Ethics: Four Views*, ed. Steve Wilkens (Downers Grove, IL: InterVarsity Press, 2017) 13.

[49] Charles H. Cosgrove, "Scripture in Ethics: A History," in *Dictionary of Scripture and Ethics*, ed. Joel B. Green (Grand Rapids: Baker, 2011), 14.

and natural law . . . have been and remain viable options within Christian ethics for centuries."[50]

However, as noted above, another viewpoint is possible. Each of these approaches appears compelling to certain people because there is something true about the moral life that each of these systems accentuates or, in some cases, exaggerates. Biblical ethics can exist at the intersection of this debate, not exactly taking sides. In fact, biblical ethics can help adjudicate some of these debates, demonstrating how some of these impulses, insights, and desires are recognized and unified by the biblical text itself.

Biblical Ethics in the Christian Life

The sort of biblical ethics we are developing here is vital for a consistent, healthy, growing, holy, sanctified Christian life. If we do not understand how God's Word provides a unified approach to ethics, we are left to our own devices to choose certain texts over others or to start out on our own in understanding what is right and wrong. We have to understand the role of the Bible and biblical ethics in the Christian life. Instead of dilemma ethics, we need a biblically formed moral imagination that leads to Holy Spirit–illuminated thoughts and behavior.

This way of phrasing the question is not the only one there is. In fact, Brian Brock reframes the question entirely: "What role does the Bible play in God's generation of a holy people? More importantly, how do we participate in this regeneration?"[51] He rightly wants us to see that if we seek a fruitful exploration of the Bible

---

[50] Wilkens, "Introduction to Four Theories," 4.

[51] Brian Brock, *Singing the Ethos of God: On the Place of Christian Ethics in Scripture* (Grand Rapids: Eerdmans, 2007), xvii.

and Christian ethics, that fruitfulness will only emerge if we see the Bible in its role in the account of God using his Word to claim and redeem humanity.[52] As we seek to understand and embody biblical ethics, we must not view ourselves going into the Bible to take what we want or need and then leaving. Instead, we must see the Bible as God's chosen and primary tool in revealing his will to his people as he shapes us into the image of his Son.

As we seek a biblical ethic, we must resist the easier, strip-mining approach. For those unfamiliar with strip-mining, precious metals located deep in mountains are a challenge to extract. In strip-mining, the top of the mountain is simply stripped off—or blown off—making the minerals easier to mine but devastating the mountain itself, the surrounding landscape, and the living ecosystem. We cannot come to the Bible as strip-miners. We do not just strip off—or blow up—the particular narrative and nature of the text, extract a few verses about a law or a moral issue, and then leave. Instead, we must recognize that the Bible is not something we handle; instead, it is God's Word, in and through which he graciously handles us, cleansing the church by the washing of the Word (Eph 5:26).

As we move now from a framework for biblical ethics into Old Testament ethics, let's listen for God's consistent voice and his work in shaping a people for himself.

---

[52] See Brock, xx.

2

The Overarching Story

Biblical ethics, as we will approach it, requires an understanding of the Bible's overarching storyline so as to hear and obey God's unified voice throughout the text. The goal here is not to hit every detail, but to have enough sense of the overall picture that we can hear God speak to us through the Bible. As Richard Bauckham puts it, "While the Bible does not have the kind of unity and coherence a single human author might give a literary work, there is nevertheless a remarkable extent to which the biblical texts themselves recognize and assert, in a necessarily cumulative manner, the unity of the story they tell."[1] Biblical ethics relies on this unity.

Other approaches get close to considering the unified voice of Scripture, but they do not go far enough. Consider this statement: "Our primary pursuit in this book is to observe the ways of

[1] Richard Bauckham, "Reading Scripture as a Coherent Story," in *The Art of Reading Scripture*, ed. Ellen F. Davis and Richard B. Hays (Grand Rapids: Eerdmans, 2003), 40.

distinguishing right from wrong that are encouraged within the biblical writings, and what rationale and motivations those writings offer for performing right activities and avoiding wrong ones."[2] Approaches like this one all too often fail to encourage the sort of across-the-canon, narrative-deepened, knowing-and-serving-God dynamics that truly undergird and make sense of all of the Bible's ethical impact. The same author gets closer to what we need with this statement: "The Bible's writings do communicate a strong sense of morals. But they do much more than that. They portray genuine ethics. They show ways of life stemming from people living in attractive relationship with the true and living God. Reasons for living morally appear regularly, either stated or implied, because relationship with God is portrayed as wonderfully good and genuinely healthy."[3] Here we get closer to the overarching story, for it is a story of a redeeming God and a redeemed people, a story that traces out over thousands of years and even into today. Living in what Peter Gosnell calls an "attractive relationship with the true and living God" is only possible through this one story.[4]

Creation

The best way to get at the heart of what the Bible says about ethics is not to search for every time the word "ethics" or "morality" is used. There are two reasons for this. First, such a search would not turn up very much. The Bible certainly mentions moral issues, and we can learn from these passages, but we need more than isolated

---

[2] Peter W. Gosnell, *The Ethical Vision of the Bible: Learning Good from Knowing God* (Downers Grove, IL: IVP Academic, 2014), 16.

[3] Gosnell, 23.

[4] Gosnell, 23.

verses. Second, such an approach might give us a few ideas about ethics, but it would not help us see the overall biblical framework that makes sense of ethics. To understand biblical ethics, we have to look to the bigger story that gives meaning to ethics—and indeed, to all of our lives.

In short, a biblical view of ethics requires us to understand an overarching biblical worldview, rooted in the broad contours of the Bible's story, the Bible's covenants, and the Bible's symbols. This is the case not because the individual passages that mention ethical issues do not matter, but because we cannot properly interpret those passages apart from this wider context. In fact, if we simply jump to the verses without the broader storyline, we are more likely to reaffirm our own preferences and previous assumptions by reading into the verses what we have internalized from our culture. We must resist proof texting without taking the story into account.[5] Rooting ourselves in a biblical worldview—incorporating the Bible's big story, covenants, and symbols—will in turn unlock the various passages that mention ethics, while also giving us eyes to see ethics in parts of the Bible we may have missed before.

If we approach the Bible as a rule book, we might think our task is to find the rules. The Bible certainly contains rules, but understanding who those rules are for, what those rules mean, and how those rules apply requires us to understand the broader context that determines their full meaning and their contribution to a biblical understanding of the world. This broader task is especially important because we know that many of today's most challenging ethical issues do not show up in the Bible. For instance, the Bible talks about children being a blessing, and there is even a

---

[5] See Gentry and Wellum, *Kingdom through Covenant*, 118 (see chap. 1, n. 14).

command—be fruitful and multiply. But it does not mention IVF, artificial wombs, or cloning. Yet, it also is not fair to say the Bible is *silent* on those issues. We must understand the Bible's overall story to make sense of such challenges.

Grasping the Bible's story sounds like a tall order, but it is not as difficult as it at first seems. Yes, the Bible was written over hundreds of years by dozens of human authors, but the one divine Author was (and is) all the time guiding his one Story to completion. At the simplest level, the Bible is about creation, fall, and redemption.[6] To expand it just a bit: God created all things. Humans sinned, resulting in disruption and disorder. God's response to that disruption was to begin immediately to repair and restore, to redeem through his own careful and patient work. In this chapter and the next, we will expand each of these three steps in turn before reflecting on the idea of the Bible's covenants and the Bible's symbols, which will give us more organizing principles for the Bible's story and in turn for biblical ethics.

When we talk about creation, we are referring to a past act, a result of that act, and a continuing act as well. Oftentimes, we think of "creation" primarily as God's original work of creation, which we learn about in Genesis 1–2. This place is, of course, the right starting point, but we will see quickly that our notion of creation must

[6] My first exposure to this idea came through reading the fine work of theologian Albert Wolters. His *Creation Regained: Biblical Basics for a Reformational Worldview* (Grand Rapids: Eerdmans, 1985) was later revised and expanded into a second edition (Grand Rapids: Eerdmans, 2005). While Wolters seeks to provide a particularly Reformed analysis of these categories, his overall treatment is simply and broadly Christian.

be expanded to account properly for the ways God relates to his creation as Creator. In other words, the idea of creation includes that God *created* and also *maintains* all that is not God (creation). As Al Wolters puts it, creation is "the correlation of the sovereign activity of the Creator and the created order."[7] So, as we explore this idea of creation, we are not only talking about the "time" in the past when God created time, space, and all there is. We are also thinking about the way that the personal God of the Bible continues to hold together, guide, and interact with what he has created.

Starting with God's original act of creation, then, puts us at the start of the Bible. There we read that in the beginning, God created the heavens and the earth (Gen 1:1). These words, "heavens" and "earth," would have communicated clearly to its original audience that God created all things. These two categories encompass and include all that exists that is not God. In particular, this view would have stood in stark contrast to other views in the ancient Near East, which saw the gods as battling each other over existing resources. The results of these disagreements and battles became the world as we see it. These accounts, such as the *Enuma Elish*, rooted all that exists, humans included, in the violence and capriciousness of the gods. It is, one could say, violence and conflict all the way down. Genesis tells us something different: there is God, and then there is everything else that exists, which exists only because God created it. And it is good.

Genesis goes on to explain how God created: by his Word. The pattern throughout verses 3–31 is God speaking, "Let there be . . ." and then that particular thing or things coming into being. God then evaluates it as good. The main interruption to this pattern comes in verses 26–31, when God creates humanity. Here the

---

[7] Wolters, 14.

pattern is paused for a moment, as God gives humans a task of dominion over the rest of creation (1:26), emphasizes their creation in his image (1:27), blesses (1:28), feeds (1:29–30), and then again evaluates the work as a whole (1:31). We will look at some of these details below when we consider the human task in light of creation and these commands.

When we look carefully at the way God speaks all things into existence, we begin to see why we cannot view creation as something that stopped on the sixth day before God rested on the seventh. We see a clue about this in verse 11. There, God calls into being "vegetation, plants yielding seed, and fruit trees bearing fruit in which is their seed" (ESV). God's very commanding-into-being of plants includes what will provide for their continued existence: seeds. Likewise, God commands the animals to be fruitful and multiply (1:22) and humans as well (1:28). God causes plants, animals, and humans not only to *be* but to *continue to be*. His command is not just for creation but for the continuity and expansion of the created order.

We might include with this creation of seeds and reproduction what we would call the "laws of nature." But consider the concept of "law" for a moment. Wolters uses "law" to "stand for the totality of God's ordaining acts toward the cosmos."[8] In other words, law encourages us to consider the various ways that God exercises his continued sovereignty over his creation, which also continues on in its created integrity (what it is), founded on and grounded in him. God lays down the law for all he has created, and this law includes what we might refer to as laws for nature and laws for humans.[9] When we are talking about the way seeds work, we are not in a

[8] Wolters, 15.

[9] Wolters uses "laws of nature" and "norms."

completely different vicinity from the law of gravity and human laws. These laws are rooted in God's creative work and his character, whether they are laws for nature or laws for humans. A longer quotation from Wolters helps us see these two types:

> There are two ways in which God imposes his law on the cosmos, two ways in which his will is done on earth as in heaven. He does it either directly, without mediation, or indirectly, through the involvement of human responsibility. Just as a human sovereign does certain things himself, but gives orders to his subordinates for other things, so with God himself. He put the planets in their orbits, makes the seasons come and go at the proper time, makes seeds grow and animals reproduce, but entrusts to mankind the tasks of making tools, doing justice, producing art, and pursuing scholarship. In other words, God's rule of law is immediate in the nonhuman realm but mediate in culture and society. In the human realm men and women become coworkers with God; as creatures made in God's image they too have a kind of lordship over the earth, are God's viceroys in creation.[10]

Wolters's language of "direct" and "indirect" provides a helpful way of thinking about all of these elements. God's law determines that plants grow. Directly. God's law also determines how humans harvest, transport, prepare, and provide food. Indirectly. God's law—his continued sovereignty—takes both of these forms.

Perhaps another biblical illustration will clarify this idea. Consider the grass. Psalm 104:14 tells us that God causes the grass to grow. This might come as a surprise to you if you remember

---

[10] Wolters, 16.

learning about photosynthesis in school. Doesn't photosynthesis cause the grass to grow? Yes, it does. Does God cause the grass to grow? Yes, he does. Photosynthesis is the scientific name we give to the process that God created and sustains for the grass to grow. This process is part of God's law. But it does not mean that God does not cause the grass to grow. It was not that all this time we thought God was involved, but once scientists discovered photosynthesis, we realized we could let God off the grass-growing job and let him work on some other things. Photosynthesis's causation does not compete with God's causation.

Humans, on the other hand, receive God's law differently. As Wolters reminds us, "The wind cannot help but obey. But human beings do have responsibility: we are held to account for the way we execute God's commandments. . . . All of human life, in all its vast array of cultural, societal, and personal relationships, is *normed* in this sense. The almighty Creator lays claim to it all."[11] The human task to follow God's law implies the indirect nature of God's law in this sense because the law works indirectly through humans. But is that so different from what we just said with the grass?

At this point, we can see where "direct" and "indirect" begin to break down, because we can notice the commonality between the way God works sovereignly over plants and over humans. God causes the grass to grow, by his law, by creating and sustaining a proper process for the plants' flourishing and growth. The grass acts appropriately to its kind by utilizing photosynthesis to grow. While Wolters would call this "direct," there is an "indirectness" to it as well: God creates the process, and God sustains the process, but the plant is still acting according to its kind. Similarly, with human actions, God created a process when he created us. We

[11] Wolters, 17.

might call this process "human freedom," by which we refer to the ability and responsibility for choosing. While we could go far afield here debating the exact definitions and extents of freedom, we will simply note that just as God causes the plant to grow, even though photosynthesis is real, God is also sovereign over human activity, even though human freedom is the proper, created process—and is real. In other words, the grass lives according to its kind, utilizing photosynthesis to grow, and we can still say "God causes the grass to grow." So with humans, who live according to our kind, utilizing freedom to live, while still affirming that God is in control and sovereign over all.

Talking about photosynthesis and human freedom seems to have led us far from the consideration of creation. But the fact that it has not is the very point. God created what he created according to its kind, creating laws for continuation and growth. God's continued creative power holds those things together and causes them to continue, whether photosynthesis or freedom. When we are talking about sovereignty or providence, we have not left the doctrine of creation but are merely recognizing the way God continues to always personally relate to the creation he has made.

These are not new ideas, and they have been articulated in various ways. Theologians have spoken of *creatio prima* to refer to God's creation of the heavens and the earth out of nothing. This idea is what we typically think of when we think of "creation." However, theologians employ the term *creatio secunda*, or "secondary creation," to refer to God's work of completing and guiding what he has created. God, through his Word, is responsible for all of this, which means that ultimately it is Christ through whom all things are created and held together (Col 1:16–17).

Let's spend a moment ensuring that we have caught what Paul was saying in Colossians 1 when he wrote clearly of Christ being before all things and holding all things together. The image that pops into my mind is Christ holding the world together—creation, its coherence, its laws. But look at the list Paul made: thrones, powers, dominions, authorities. Now, scholars have debated what these terms refer to precisely, but at the very least they are gesturing toward more than just holding flowers and seasons and gravity together. Thrones, powers, dominions, authorities. All are rightly held together by Christ and submitted to him for his glory.

Moving beyond what we typically think of with the created order, we must also reflect on how God's creation includes what we would typically put under the heading of "ethics." What is right, what is wrong; all is rooted in the laws of God in creation. As Wolters puts it, "Human civilization is *normed* throughout. Everywhere we discover limits and proprieties, standards and criteria: in every field of human affairs there are right and wrong ways of doing things. There is nothing in human life that does not belong to the created order."[12] In other words, when talking about right and wrong, we mean not only moral issues or potential sins but also the right way of living and moving and being within God's created order. We often use "wisdom" to refer to this broader sense of knowing and operating within right and wrong.

Creation also includes the "creation mandate," when God commands people to fill, subdue, and rule over the rest of creation (Gen 1:28). Humans are commanded to steward God's work, according to the way he has created, and to extend the visibility of his rule throughout the world. Just as other aspects of creation were created to flourish through the laws God created (photosynthesis, from our

---

[12] Wolters, 25.

earlier discussion), so also humans are meant to flourish by working along with God's laws in their oversight of creation.

We have already seen some of this in relation to the creation mandate—the commands God gave humans when he created them. Be fruitful, multiple, fill the earth, subdue it. But we can expand on this idea by looking at how the creation and the creation mandate communicate the idea that creation is not primarily a playground for humans. The creation mandate, the laws of right and wrong, and all the other elements of God's creation are not there simply as a grand experiment to see what humans might do. Rather, it is all directed to the ultimate good: humans' recognition of and worship of God's glory in relationship with him.

In this view, creation was meant to serve as God's temple, a place for displaying his glory. New Testament scholar Greg Beale develops this idea extensively in his *The Temple and the Church's Mission: A Biblical Theology of the Dwelling Place of God.*[13] Beale argues that the signs of God's presence in the Old Testament—the tabernacle and the temple, especially—point forward to the reality of God's presence in the end times. In fact, this symbolism did not start with the tabernacle but with the garden of Eden itself, which "was the first archetypal temple in which the first man worshipped God."[14] The garden of Eden was the unique place where God was present in his new creation, Adam served as a sort of priest, and various elements of the later temple have precursors in the garden. When we look at creation and the garden of Eden, we see that the

---

[13] G. K. Beale, *The Temple and the Church's Mission: A Biblical Theology of the Dwelling Place of God* (Downers Grove, IL: InterVarsity, 2004).

[14] Beale, 66.

realities of the garden and the tasks given to Adam only make sense in light of this notion of God's presence.

Understanding this temple context provides another angle for considering the reality of God's creation and humanity's task within it. Adam's role is to keep and guard the garden. This activity is a priestly one, with connections to later biblical passages. When we view humanity's task this way, we see that all of it is oriented toward worship. Adam's task was to work to protect and expand the temple so that God's presence might shine forth throughout all of creation. As Beale puts it, "In actuality, Adam, as God's vice-regent, and his progeny were to put 'the finishing touches' on the world God created in Genesis 1 by making it a livable place for humans. . . . God's ultimate goal in creation was to magnify his glory throughout the earth by means of his faithful image bearers inhabiting the world in obedience to the divine mandate."[15] Furthermore, Beale explains the view in the ancient Near East of temples being expanded through the rule of priest-kings who were in the image of the deity.[16] It was common for ancient kings to put "images" of themselves in distant lands to remind people who the ruler was, to signify and extend that ruler's presence and authority. The language related to the garden of Eden, of Adam and Eve as created in God's image, and of the tasks given to them, are rich with connections to this notion that the original hearers and readers of this text would have recognized. In other words, Adam's task to keep and guard also included expanding the garden-as-symbol-of-God's-presence out into the rest of creation. All that he did was meant to have this as its goal: to make clear to the world who its true Lord is. To guide all of creation into recognition of and worship of God's glory.

---

[15] Beale, 82.

[16] See Beale, 87.

Clearly, a fuller picture of God's creation work gives us a foundation upon which to consider biblical ethics. We see that God created humans and put them in a world that had laws and ways things worked, including the plants and the people. God also gave them a task: to keep the garden that symbolized his rule and to extend that sense of his presence to all of creation. Even with only this, we can begin to jump to ways that biblical ethics draws on and explains this task. However, if we start reflecting on ethics now, we will miss out on a key feature of the story that warns us against ways we could quickly go wrong.

The Fall

Although God's creation was good, evil and distortion emerged through Adam and Eve's sin. God gave this first couple a clear mandate to serve as his image bearers and to extend his rule graciously through and beyond the garden of Eden. Along with this command, God gave one prohibition: do not eat of the tree of the knowledge of good and evil (Gen 2:17). One interpretation of the reasoning of this rule is that God wanted them to trust his word and obey him, focusing attention on his absolute lordship. In other words, "Adam and Eve must learn to obey for no other reason than because God says so."[17] If they disobeyed, they would die.

---

[17] Michael W. Goheen and Craig G. Bartholomew, *Living at the Crossroads: An Introduction to Christian Worldview* (Grand Rapids: Baker, 2008), 46.

Adam and Eve soon found themselves faced with a choice, prodded by an enterprising, evil snake. Satan appeared to Eve, questioned the veracity of God's word, and encouraged her to break God's law. She, along with Adam, took of the fruit and ate (Gen 3:1–6). We immediately see the effects of this: the couple realize their nakedness, seek to cover themselves, and hide from God (Gen 3:7–8).

The punishment for their sin was swift and clear. God no longer allowed them to eat of the tree of life (thus, they begin the long walk toward death) and banished them from the garden of Eden. This affected all of life. Their relationship with each other will involve new strains (Gen 3:16). Their relationship with the world around them will be more difficult (childbearing in Gen 3:16; toilsome working of the ground in Gen 3:17–18). The only hope is that God also promises to send someone, a promised Seed (child), who will crush the serpent's head (Gen 3:15). The narrative immediately turns to this promise, with Adam naming the woman "Eve" because she will be the mother of all living, and then tells us about her offspring. The point is clear: after the fall, everything revolves around waiting for the promised child who will make things right.

While familiar with this part of the story, we should pause to note the barrier the fall places between the first couple and their work. They were meant to extend the garden as a visible sign of God's presence, but instead of extending they have been expelled. Not only will their task of imaging God become much more complicated as a result, but everything gets harder.

If you have thought about the impact of the fall before, you have likely made the connections above, which the text makes obvious. However, theologians have extended our thinking about the effects of the fall by considering the implications the fall had for the way we come to know and understand things. The humans' failure to obey meant being expelled from the garden, where they had close relationship with God and were taught by him. The fall impacts not only our actions but also our intellect and capacities. This idea is often referred to as the "noetic" effects of the fall. At this stage in our exploration, we need to be careful even about our own thinking and knowing, praying that God will renew our hearts *and* our minds. We cannot assume that everything we think we know is right or that we have interpreted the world in the right way. We need God's revelation to help us understand rightly, to overcome these noetic effects of the fall through the Word of God by the power and grace of the Spirit of God.

The fall not only impaired humans but also altered the way the world works. We have seen a hint of this already in the way the fall changed work: the fruit of the ground would be more difficult to obtain. Thorns and thistles would wreak their havoc. In short, humans were tasked with being God's representatives over the world, and their first failure in that task had massive implications for that world. This idea is what Paul refers to when he says that the entire created world is "groaning" while it waits for redemption, for the sons of God to be revealed (Rom 8:22). Brokenness. "Wherever anything wrong exists in the world, anything we experience as antinormative, evil, distorted, or sick, there we meet the perversion of God's good creation."[18] The story runs from their sin to the Tower of Babel, with fratricide (Gen 4:8), polygamy (Gen 4:19), murder and revenge (Gen 4:23), and the flood, which is aimed at human wickedness, and continues even among Noah and

[18] Wolters, *Creation Regained*, 55.

his sons. In short, the first chapters of Genesis show the darkness of the world after Adam and Eve's sin.[19]

We might be tempted to think that this fall business is a bit of an overreaction to one simple little sin. But when we recall what we learned in the previous chapter about God's creation and the law he created and embedded in it, we see better that sin is first and foremost against God. Michael Goheen and Craig Bartholomew helpfully draw out this truth, noting that Paul sees the religious allegiance in play in human history: "They exchanged the truth of God for a lie, and worshiped and served the created things rather than the Creator" (Rom 1:25 NIV). They further explain that humans will find something to put at the center of their lives—an idol—whenever they reject God.[20] We must not minimize the rebellion of sin or its results.

One of the most helpful ways to consider a Christian view of the world as a result of the fall is with the ideas of "structure" and "direction." Introduced by Wolters, these terms help us see the goodness of what God originally created (the structure of all creation) while also recognizing that the structure of creation can move toward God or away from God (the direction of creation). As he puts it, structure "is anchored in the law of creation . . . [and] designates a reality that the philosophical tradition of the West has often referred to by such words as *substance*, *essence*, and *nature*."[21] Direction, on the other hand, "designates the order of sin and redemption, the distortion or perversion of creation through the fall on the one hand and the redemption and restoration

---

[19] See Goheen and Bartholomew, *Living at the Crossroads*, 46.

[20] See Goheen and Bartholomew, 47.

[21] Wolters, *Creation Regained*, 59.

of creation in Christ on the other. Anything in creation can be directed either toward or away from God."[22] This structure and direction distinction reminds us of central truths about creation. It was created good. The fall introduced sin, which impacted not only humans but all of creation. It is all bent the wrong way, causing pain, evil, and suffering. But this distinction also reminds us that this is not the case because of creation but because of the fall: "We have seen that the fall affects the whole range of earthly creation; that sin is a parasite on, and not a part of, creation; and that, to the degree that it affects the whole earth, sin profanes all things, making them 'worldly,' 'secular,' 'earthly.' Consequently, every area of the created world cries out for redemption and the coming of the kingdom of God."[23]

By grace alone, God did not end the story with the fall. Instead, as we see in Genesis 3, God promised both very real punishments and very real deliverance. As mentioned above, after the fall, everything centers on waiting and hoping for this promised Seed who will defeat evil. What God commands only makes sense in light of this promise. God does not say, "Everything is broken; figure out how to fix it." Rather, he tells Adam and Eve that life will be harder: they will no longer be in the garden, childbirth will be painful, working the ground will be difficult. Life will be harder. But God did not leave them to their own devices to figure out what to do. And, sitting where we are after God's promised Seed has come, we know that even the promised Seed does not defeat evil by humanity's own machinations, but by being fully God and fully man. Though the person and work of Christ are not clearly revealed in

---

[22] Wolters, 59.

[23] Wolters, 67–68.

Genesis 3, God does point in that direction. This "protoevangelion" or "first gospel" makes God's plan clear: redemption.

Redemption

God's reaction to sin was immediate. In Genesis 3, he pronounced clear consequences for the serpent, the woman, the man, and their progeny. However, nestled in those pronouncements of judgment is not only the first sign of hope but a sign of God's commitment to accomplish redemption at great cost. He speaks of the woman's offspring, a promised Seed who would rise up. The text says that the serpent would strike his heel but the offspring would crush the serpent's head (Gen 3:15). We can quickly pass by this "first gospel," but we shouldn't. As a prophecy, it predicts the ultimate defeat of evil. As a promise, it makes sure and certain that the problems introduced by the fall will be solved.

From Gen 3:15 onward, the Bible's storyline is following this promise, seeking to answer the question, "Who is this promised one?" While we cannot go into great detail in this section, we will attempt to cover major sections in the story to make sense of the whole. From Genesis 4–11, we realize that this Seed might not come right away and crush evil. We see conflict between brothers, violence between budding nations, God punishing evil with the flood, and evil's continued growth even in the family of Noah. Ultimately, we see the Tower of Babel, a human attempt to construct a bridge between the earthly and divine realms (Genesis 11). At each turn, readers are confronted with the reality that this promised Seed has not yet arrived to defeat evil.

When God calls Abram in Genesis 12, we begin to see some of the shape of God's plan for this Seed. God calls one man and makes a covenant with him. One element to highlight here, before discussing it in more detail in the next chapter: God promises to bless the entire world through the offspring of this man. We should immediately notice that this promise sounds tied to the promise made to Adam and Eve, and indeed we see that God does intend to bring that Seed through Abraham's descendants.

A deep dive into the Old Testament would turn up disappointment after disappointment as God's people (and readers) wait for this promised Seed and this blessing to the nations. We see remarkable ways that God makes part of the promise come true, giving us a preview of what the ultimate fulfillment will look like. Joseph, for instance, in the latter chapters of Genesis, proves to be a blessing to Egypt as he prepares them to survive a famine. But he brings God's people out of the land of promise, into a land of (what would end up being) captivity. Moses himself, though a great leader of God's people, struggles with the faith to believe God's word and ultimately dies before the people reenter the Promised Land. Each judge demonstrates not only God's ability to raise up a leader to deliver his people but also the people's swiftness in returning to sin. Israel's first three kings—Saul, David, and Solomon—each show flashes of being the promised Seed, bringing true blessing. Saul unites the people and brings some military victories but fails in the long run. David demonstrates great faith, brings God's people the peace and prosperity God promised, but ultimately fails because of his own sin. Solomon seems to get so close: leaders from around the world travel to him to be blessed by his wisdom; we see Solomon being a blessing to the nations. But he fails too. As Israel splits into the northern and southern kingdoms, king after king demonstrates complete corruption, and despite some faithfulness, the kings are ultimately unable to usher in the promises that God made.

As the Old Testament draws to a close, we find the people of God wrestling to remain faithful in the midst of these repeated failures. For it was not only the leaders who failed, but the people who rushed off into sin. As Israel was ultimately led into exile and then ruled over by foreign powers, the theological problem was palpable. Even the prophets always reminded the Israelites that they needed to respond faithfully to the story and the covenant.[24] The God of Israel had made certain promises; if he was the true God, why did those promises seem so far away, so impossible? We cannot understand first-century Israel without understanding that this theological problem lay heavily on the people, and different groups proposed different answers to it.

After 400 years of silence, Jesus enters this stage of the Bible's story. The Gospel writers all present him as the fulfillment of promises God made in the Old Testament. Jesus lives the perfect life, demonstrating what true human flourishing should look like. He teaches about the kingdom of God, announcing its arrival and calling people to this new reality. Not every Israelite received Jesus and his ministry in the same way, of course. Some were waiting for a certain type of deliverance, a certain type of Messiah. While Jesus did not fit those expectations (he did not overthrow Roman rule, for instance), he did fulfill all that the Old Testament promised. The Second Person of the Trinity, fully God, took on everything it means to be human. The promised Seed of the woman had arrived.

Not only did Jesus teach about the kingdom of God; he achieved its arrival through his sacrificial death on the cross. Christians think regularly about Jesus's death on the cross as the payment or substitution for human sin. This concept is vital to our understanding of what Jesus died for. He died to make possible reconciliation between sinners and God. This has obvious

---

[24] See Verhey, "Ethics in Scripture," 6 (see chap. 1, n. 9).

implications for the story so far because it enables humans to live rightly in fellowship with God again. But it is also relevant for all of creation. This relevance is established and made firm by Christ's resurrection. His resurrection signifies many things, including his divinity, the trustworthiness of his teaching and promises, and his eternal identity as the true Davidic king. These implications matter not only for the humans who believe in him and are thus "in Christ," but also for all of creation, which Christ is renewing. As Bartholomew and Goheen explain, Jesus's death for the entire world settles the course of cosmic history, and New Testament writers saw the end-time kingdom beginning at this point in a very real way.[25] Allen Verhey reminds us, "The resurrection was a cause for great joy; it was also the basis for NT ethics and its exhortations to live in memory and in hope, to see moral conduct and character in the light of Jesus' story, and to discern a life and a common life 'worthy of the gospel of Jesus Christ' (Phil. 1:27)."[26] The kingdom has arrived, and that matters for humans and for all of the created world, even as we continue to wait for the fullness of that kingdom.

After Jesus's resurrection and ascension, he sent the Holy Spirit as he promised to his people. The Holy Spirit makes real the idea that the kingdom is indeed here but that we wait for its fullness. Theologians refer to these as the "already" and the "not yet" aspects of the kingdom. The Holy Spirit is "not only a promise of the future kingdom but also a real gift here and now. The salvation of God's kingdom is really experienced in the Spirit's present work—its joy, *shalom*, righteousness, and knowledge of God—and he also carries the pledge of God that the fullness of God's gracious reign is yet to

[25] See Goheen and Bartholomew, *Living at the Crossroads*, 56.

[26] Verhey, "Ethics in Scripture," 7.

come."[27] God is working now, gathering a people who trust in the work of the Son.

These gathered people take on a special task as the world waits for Christ to return. In short, the church provides witness to the kingdom of God, both its "already" and its "not yet." The church speaks the truth of the inbreaking kingdom of God by pointing to the work of Christ on the cross and urging people to repent and trust in Christ. The church also shows the truth of the kingdom of God by showing what life in that kingdom is meant to look like. Thus, the moral witness of the church does not achieve or earn salvation but points to the goodness of the kingdom of God. The church clothes the naked and feeds the hungry because by doing so it points forward to the kingdom of God, where no one will be cold or hungry. Doing these things provides some of the "already" of the kingdom and points forward to the "not yet" of the kingdom.

The New Testament provides not only instructions for the church but also eschatological pictures of a renewed creation. For instance, God reconciles *all things* to himself in Christ (Col 1:19–20), bringing all things in heaven and on earth under the headship of Christ (Eph 1:9–10), so that in the end God will indeed make all things new (Rev 21:5). Even while the church focuses on preaching the gospel with words, its kingdom-oriented actions also bear witness to this eschatological reality of the entire world being renewed, being made new in Christ. Thus, briefly, we can gesture to the fact that the church should take an interest in caring for the created world because doing so is one way that it serves as a sign pointing forward to the "not yet" renewal of all things.

---

[27] Goheen and Bartholomew, *Living at the Crossroads*, 57.

Redemption is progressive, restorative, and comprehensive. In other words, though it will take time, complete restoration will happen. Sin and its effects are being overcome, even while we wait for that ultimate restoration brought in with the return of the enthroned king, Jesus Christ. In the meantime, we must remember that the problem is not the creation, but sin. As Bartholomew and Goheen remind us, "The materiality of creation is not what is wrong with it; the problem is sin."[28] This fact helps us see that biblical ethics should never seek to escape our embodiment or flee creation; that will not solve the problem. But we are getting ahead of ourselves; we will revisit that idea later in the book.

How can we draw all of this together? How can we properly understand God's good creation, its distortion due to human sin, and the already-and-not-yet nature of the redemption accomplished by Christ? Again, Goheen and Bartholomew provide help here. They give two illustrations for understanding the relationship between creation, sin, and redemption. First, they note that creation is like an earthly kingdom that has been overtaken by a usurper, Satan. The original ruler, God, undertakes a long campaign to reclaim the kingdom. The battle is ongoing, though the ending is certain. Second, they use the example of a healthy newborn, complete yet full of potential. When the child contracts a disease, the doctor must treat the child of the disease, ridding the body of the problem even while the young child grows and develops. As they explain, "The doctor's remedy is meant not to destroy the child or make her something different than she had been but rather to destroy the

[28] Goheen and Bartholomew, 53.

disease so that she might again be healthy. That is the way God's healing work takes place. He does not destroy the creation, nor does he turn it into something different; the whole work of salvation is meant to remove the sin that has sickened the creation and to restore it (and us) to health."[29] Both of these illustrations helpfully highlight the dynamic between something that is good and right but has been corrupted and distorted. Each illustrates well the idea of "structure" and "direction" that Wolters uses and that we explored earlier.

God's love in promising redemption connects to the specific arrangements he makes with people in what the Bible calls "covenants." In fact, the covenants provide something of the plot for the entire "redemption" section of the Bible's story.

---

[29] Goheen and Bartholomew, 63.

3

Covenants and Redemption

The "redemption" stage of the Bible's story is long and varied. You might argue that having that entire part of the story under one heading makes the "creation-fall-redemption" rubric less useful, but that is not the case when we properly understand it. The simplicity of those three steps is helpful and true: God created, humans distorted it all, and God redeemed (and is redeeming) it. Everything that occurs from Genesis 3 to Revelation 21 is part of God's one, unified, successful plan of redemption. The key here is that we do not have a series of God's failed attempts, or a series of the Father's best tries until he finally stumbles upon the idea of sending the Second Person of the Trinity to dwell among us. Rather, we have a pattern that establishes God as a good and loving God who delights in showing his love through making and keeping covenants. Further, God ordered history and culture around his design at creation.[1] Every step of the way in God's work of redemption, he follows a unified plan that points backward to the goodness of creational design and forward to his ultimate work in Christ.

The most helpful way to understand how God works redemption is to use the Bible's covenants as guideposts for comprehending the cohesion of God's plan. This will in turn help us to better understand biblical ethics. The kingdom of God comes through the covenants. What is a covenant? It is "a chosen relationship in which two parties make binding promises to each other."[2] In the Bible, "['Covenant'] is used to refer to international treaties (Josh. 9:6; 1 Kings 15:19), clan alliances (Gen. 14:13), personal agreements (Gen. 31:44), national agreements (Jer. 34:8–10), and loyalty agreements (1 Sam. 20:14–16), including marriage (Mal. 2:14)."[3] But when we speak of the Bible's covenants, we are referring to the major covenants that God makes with key representatives of humanity—people like Noah and Abraham.

Biblical scholar Peter Gentry and systematic theologian Stephen Wellum make a comprehensive case for this idea in their book *Kingdom through Covenant: A Biblical-Theological Understanding of the Covenants*. They argue that God's kingdom comes through covenants in two ways. First, it comes through the relationships that God establishes with those created in his image, relationships he establishes using covenants.[4] Second, God's kingdom coming through covenants reminds us that this kingdom comes over time,

---

[1] See Goheen and Bartholomew, *Living at the Crossroads*, 55 (see chap. 2, n. 17).

[2] Schreiner, *40 Questions*, 13 (see chap. 1, n. 39).

[3] Gentry and Wellum, *Kingdom through Covenant*, 163 (see chap. 1, n. 14). Used by permission of Crossway, a publishing ministry of Good News Publishers, Wheaton, IL 60187, www.crossway.org.

[4] See Gentry and Wellum, 34.

building and becoming clearer through Noah, Abraham, Israel, David, and ultimately, Jesus.[5]

The covenants bind the Bible's various stories into one unified plot.[6] In what follows we will seek a basic sense of each of these main covenants in order to better understand this unified plot and how it provides a more promising way to think about biblical ethics.

Creation Covenant

The first covenant in the Bible begins the pattern of God's love made manifest through making and keeping promises. Scholars are at odds as to whether there really is a covenant at creation, mainly because the Bible does not say explicitly, "And God made a covenant with Adam." Such clear statements are common features of the other biblical covenants we will explore. However, rather than going into the depths of the exegetical arguments on each side, we will rely on Gentry and Wellum's conclusions to guide us. Their treatment of the cultural background and exegetical research leads them to rely on the fact that there are many expressions in the Bible and in the ancient Near East that were used to refer to covenants without using the word "covenant." "Image" and "likeness" are those words in Genesis 1–3. In fact, "the term 'the image of god' in the culture and language of the ancient Near East in the fifteenth century BC would have communicated two main ideas: (1) rulership and (2) sonship. The king is the image of god because he has a relationship to the deity as the son of god and a relationship to the world as ruler for the god."[7] In creating man in his own

[5] See Gentry and Wellum, 34–35.

[6] See Gentry and Wellum, 171.

[7] See Gentry and Wellum, 238.

image and giving him a task, we also see God draw alongside Adam and Eve, showing that God is not only transcendent, he also comes alongside; God is "with us."[8] Additionally, we must understand these relationships as covenants because that is how the original culture would have understood them, and we shouldn't reject that meaning unless there is a clear reason to do so.[9] In other words, even if the Bible does not use the word "covenant," God can still communicate, "This is a covenant" by using words like "image" and "likeness," which would have indicated a covenant in their original context.[10]

What we see then with the creation covenant is that the ideas we explored in the previous chapter—especially related to the task Adam was given at creation—are rooted in covenant from the very beginning. When we hear "image of God," we must understand this as a covenantal relationship.[11] Also, all the other covenants on the Bible are built upon and unpack this covenant.[12] We will see this notion continue with the next covenant.

Covenant with Noah

God's covenant with Noah is arguably the most famous because of its covenant sign: the rainbow. As Genesis tells us, God responded to the world's increasing wickedness by sending a flood. He saved one righteous man, Noah, and his family by telling them to build an ark. This ark saved them and their animal passengers from

---

[8] Graham A. Cole, *The God Who Became Human: A Biblical Theology of Incarnation* (Downers Grove, IL: IVP Academic, 2013), 33.

[9] See Gentry and Wellum, *Kingdom through Covenant*, 227.

[10] See Schreiner, *40 Questions*, 20.

[11] Gentry and Wellum, *Kingdom through Covenant*, 236.

[12] See Gentry and Wellum, 672.

certain death. After the flood waters receded, God made a covenant with Noah, promising never again to flood the earth. He put his bow in the clouds as a sign of that covenant, which he promised without exception.

While some theologians prefer to speak of this covenant as an unconditional covenant, conditional and unconditional are not helpful categories for covenants. They are unhelpful because even a clearly unconditional covenant like the one with Noah calls for particular actions and insists on stewardship.[13] Yes, God promised never again to flood the earth. There is no "condition" that would cause this promise to end or fall through. However, "unconditional" communicates that there is no right response or requirement on the part of God's creation.

One of the first elements of the story with Noah requires interpretation within the broader covenantal context of creation. In Gen 9:1–6, God prohibits murder, setting up the penalty of death for anyone who murders a fellow human. In verse 6, God roots this command and penalty in the fact that he created humans in his own image. This clue tells us we must understand this aspect of the covenant with Noah not only in light of creation but in light of the entire story of Noah and the flood.

To rightly understand this particular covenant, we have to connect it to the covenant that God made at creation. The way God speaks of his covenant with Noah shows that he extends his previous commitment, made at creation, to Noah and his family.[14] In other words, we can see the flood as a new creation and Noah as a new Adam. The terminology God uses in making this covenant connects it to a previous promise. It is not that this is a covenant

[13] See Gentry and Wellum, 207.

[14] See Gentry and Wellum, 195.

renewal, but it is also not a brand-new, out-of-nowhere, additional covenant. It is rooted in the previous one.

This covenant, and the fact that God will never again flood the earth, sets up the rest of Genesis and the rest of the Bible. As Gentry and Wellum put it, "The unmerited favor and kindness of God in preserving his world in the covenant with Noah creates a firm stage of history where God can work out his plan for rescuing the fallen world. It also points ahead to the coming deliverance in Jesus Christ."[15] It is on this firm stage that God makes his next covenant, with Abraham.

Covenant with Abraham

After God's covenant with Noah, it becomes exceedingly clear that sin will continue to be a problem. We see this before Noah's story even ends: his drunkenness and his sons' behavior show that even this "righteous man" falls short. After the debacle of the Tower of Babel, God focuses his redemptive plans on one man, Abram. Abram becomes another Adam, a place where God makes a new start.[16]

God calls Abram to leave his land for an as-yet-undisclosed location. From that point, we see God's relationship with Abram grow and develop. God made promises to Abraham in Genesis 12, and then put those promises in covenantal form in Genesis 15 and 17. Through this period, we see Abraham grow in faith.[17] God makes six promises to Abram, which we can split into two groups. The first group of promises are about blessings for Abram himself—he will become a great nation, be blessed, and receive

---

[15] Gentry and Wellum, 208. Used with permission.

[16] See Gentry and Wellum, 260.

[17] See Gentry and Wellum, 264–65.

a great name. The second group are about blessing for the world through Abram—those who bless Abram will be blessed; those who curse him will be cursed; God will bless all the clans of the earth through this one family. As it becomes clear, the promises are related: the first three promises are the root of the final three; God's plan to bless Abraham and his offspring brings blessing and salvation to others.[18] In short, God will use this family as the instrument for rescuing the creation.[19]

If Abraham is to become a great nation, he needs land. This "Promised Land" is not an end in itself but is tied to becoming a great nation, which in turn is tied to being a blessing to the entire world. Even the location of the Promised Land connects to these ideas. Gentry and Wellum liken the Promised Land to the "central spine of the Internet" of the ancient world because everything flowed through that piece of land. Those passing through should see there the people of God on display—worshipping the one true God, obeying his law, and being good stewards.[20] This passage highlights well that the entire covenant with Abraham makes sense in light of the previous covenants, especially the promise that God has made to send a redeemer and to overcome sin.

Are we beginning to get a pattern of God starting over again and again? Wasn't Noah a new start too? Should we expect another? Gentry and Wellum answer, "God makes another new start, with Abram and his family. Abraham and his family, called Israel, are another Adam, who will be God's true humanity. The seed of Abraham, Israel, is in fact the last Adam because there will be no major new starts for humanity from this point. Israel will display

---

[18] See Gentry and Wellum, 279.

[19] See Gentry and Wellum, 270–71.

[20] Gentry and Wellum, 297–98.

to the rest of the world within its covenant community the kind of relationships—first to God and then to one another—as well as stewardship of the ecosystem, that God originally intended for all humanity."[21] These promises made to Abraham form the basis for God's dealings with humans going forward.[22]

Mosaic Covenant

After God brings the Israelites out of Egypt, he makes a covenant with them. The idea is that he wants them to enjoy blessings even as they become a blessing to all nations. We might be tempted to view the Mosaic covenant as primarily a bunch of rules that the people have to keep if they want to maintain their status as God's people. While the Ten Commandments and other laws carry with them consequences for disobedience, and the entire sacrificial system is built to maintain their connection with God despite their sin, we must remember that God desires to bless this people and to make them a blessing to others.

How does God do that? We can view the Mosaic covenant as a covenant highlighting for the people what true human flourishing looks like. It shows these people how to be truly human, how to relate to God in the right way, and how to relate to others too. It even shows them how to relate to the world around them by being faithful stewards of what God has made.[23] Again, the covenant is meant not to catch them in their sin but to bless Israel and to bless through Israel, connecting the Mosaic covenant to the Abrahamic covenant.

---

[21] Gentry and Wellum, 283. Used with permission.

[22] See Gentry and Wellum, 332.

[23] See Gentry and Wellum, 342.

The covenant looks sort of like an international treaty of the time. International treaties followed a form: preamble, historical prologue, stipulations, and document clause.[24] In the covenant, God calls the people a "kingdom of priests" and a "holy nation," both of which connect to the idea of being a light to the nations. The ideas of kingdom of priests and a holy nation are both tied to the Abrahamic covenant. This speaks of being devoted to God, but also of serving as a light to the nations.[25] The purpose of their priesthood and holiness is not exclusive but bound up with the promise to make them a blessing to all nations.

We can see this in the Ten Commandments. In short, the Ten Commandments show that the covenant with Moses rightly orders people's relationship with God, and also human relationships.[26] In other words, these commands are meant to show how to live rightly with God and with one another, in both an individual context and, by extension, in a community.

It is more helpful to consider this covenant and its laws as a whole rather than dividing them into categories and trying to decide which matter for today. We cannot break the law up into moral, civil, and ceremonial laws and just apply one (a tempting choice for Christians trying to understand the law); this misunderstands the overall nature of the covenant and what it is actually doing. Though many scholars who take this approach

---

[24] See Gentry and Wellum, 346. More specifically, "The covenant is formulated as a suzerain-vassal treaty in order to define God as Father and King and Israel as obedient son in a relationship of loyal love, obedience, and trust." Used with permission of Crossway. See also Meredith Kline, *The Treaty of the Great King: The Covenant Structure of Deuteronomy* (Grand Rapids: Eerdmans, 1963), 13.

[25] See Gentry and Wellum, 356–65.

[26] See Gentry and Wellum, 365.

attempt to situate their positions in ways that avoid this misunderstanding, this nuance can be lost on other Christians trying to apply the division. Plus, "this classification is foreign to the material and imposed on it from the outside rather than arising from the material and being clearly marked by the literary structure of the text."[27] It might seem straightforward to claim that the "moral" parts still matter, while the "civil" is time bound and the entire ceremonial law is "fulfilled" in Christ. Such distinctions can help us see important matters, but ultimately those issues are not present in the Mosaic text itself. Rather, they come out when we properly understand the law in light of the overall story culminating in Christ. In other words, we do not determine that certain laws fit a category and therefore do not apply; instead, we understand what is actually happening in the overall story of Scripture and thereby understand better the way these commands make claims on us.

Now that we have considered briefly the Ten Commandments and the structure of the covenant overall, we can look at what some scholars call the key text in the Mosaic covenant or, indeed, in the entire Old Testament: Deut 6:4–9.[28] Deuteronomy is the center of the Old Testament, the climax of the Pentateuch. The command in 6:5 is the center, where the Israelites are commanded to love God with all their heart, soul, and strength.[29] Jesus calls this the greatest commandment (Matt 22:36–40). It reminds us that this whole covenant is rooted in reestablishing a right relationship with God through blessing Israel and making Israel a blessing to the nations. This extension of relationship with God can be understood as an

---

[27] Gentry and Wellum, 393. Used with permission.

[28] See Gentry and Wellum, 397.

[29] See discussion in Gentry and Wellum, 405–10.

extension of God's rightful rule, which of course returns us to the original role that God gave Adam. In fact, the exodus is a fulfillment of God's covenant with Abraham, and Exod 19:5–6 shows that God wants the nation to fulfill the Adamic role reassigned to Abraham through observing the Mosaic covenant.[30]

Davidic Covenant

The next biblical covenant is with Israel's greatest king, David. The beginning of 2 Samuel tells us about David's great success, which is why he wants to build a "house" for God, a permanent temple. What follows in 2 Samuel 7 is referred to as the Davidic covenant. In short, God flips the script and tells David that he will build a house—an eternal dynasty—for the king. We see this in three main passages: 2 Samuel 7, 1 Chronicles 17, and Psalm 89. But what does this covenant mean, and how is it kept?

First, we must connect this covenant to the ones God has already made. Humans are created in the divine image, and Israel inherited the Adamic role. Further, the king of Israel will be leader in this role.[31] The Davidic covenant shows a new model of kingship for God's people and also demonstrates God's kingship at a new level. It carries forward God's intentions and purposes shown in previous covenants too.[32]

Because of this connection between the covenants, we see that that Davidic covenant is also tied into God's grace to the entire world, not just to David. This is because the faithfulness of David connects to God's rule over the whole world, just as God intended

[30] See Gentry and Wellum, 442.

[31] See Gentry and Wellum, 455–56.

[32] See Gentry and Wellum, 443.

for humanity created in his image.[33] The promised Seed of the covenant with Abraham—as plentiful as the stars in the sky—is inherited by David's seed.[34] The promises of this covenant are divided in two. Some are fulfilled in David's lifetime—a great name, the place for Israel as God's people, and safety from enemies. Others are fulfilled later—the "eternal house," kingdom, and throne. Even with this brief treatment of the covenant with David, we can see the way it is connected with and grows out of the previous covenants, all of which are aimed at solving the problem of sin introduced in the fall.

Gentry and Wellum summarize well the way these covenants fit together. We must understand these connections before we move on to understand the new covenant: "God responds to human rebellion in various ways as the story unfolds. As we have seen, at the center of a plan to restore his ruined world and bring it to serve his original intentions are a series of agreements called covenants."[35] The Noahic covenant shows God's commitment to the whole creation. Then, in the Abrahamic covenant, God starts working through one individual, to model a new humanity through his family that relates rightly to God and to one another. Then, the Mosaic covenant defines the people of God and guides their life in the Promised Land. The covenant with David creates a form of kingship that better establishes God among his people because the king functions as the administrator of the covenant. The king leads and implements what God has planned.[36] The thread continues through David and prepares us for the new covenant.

---

[33] See Gentry and Wellum, 457.

[34] See Gentry and Wellum, 485.

[35] Gentry and Wellum, 487.

[36] See Gentry and Wellum, 487.

New Covenant

As the rest of the Old Testament shows, the Israelites, and even the kings, do not exactly excel at holding up their end of the covenant. The role of the prophets is to continually call people back to the stipulations of the covenant, which the people fail to uphold. Because of the repeated failure, the prophets begin to reveal that God plans a new covenant—one where he will be faithful and will cause his people to be faithful as well. This new covenant is not different from the old but fulfills them all.[37] This is not Plan B, but the culmination of God's one plan of redemption.

Various texts deal with the idea of a new covenant. Some speak of an everlasting covenant (Isa 55:1–5; 61:8–9; Jer 32:36–41; 50:2–5; Ezek 37:15–28). Others mention a covenant of peace (Isa 54:1–10; Ezek 34:20–31; 37:15–28). A third idea is the promise of a new heart and a new spirit (Ezek 11:18–21; 18:30–32; 36:24–32). Jeremiah 31:31–34 is the only passage that uses the exact term "new covenant" to cover these ideas.[38] All of these texts revolve around the idea that, in the new covenant, God will obey on the people's behalf and make it possible for them to obey and live in righteousness. Again, if we consider the covenants as connected together and rooted in God's plan for salvation for the world, we see the importance of this.

Ultimately, the new covenant is inaugurated and established by Jesus Christ, the Son of God. The Second Person of the Trinity took on flesh, lived a perfect life, taught about the reality of the kingdom, died for sins, rose on the third day, and ascended into heaven, from which he rules and will return. Jesus also sent the

---

[37] See Gentry and Wellum, 660.

[38] See Gentry and Wellum, 488.

Holy Spirit, who brings about the new birth, the new heart, the new spirit, and the obedience the prophets spoke about. This is the covenant we are called to take part in today, through faith in Christ. But even this covenant is connected to and only makes sense through the others.

Gentry and Wellum highlight important ways that the new covenant is like the old. First, the new covenant is the answer to hard-heartedness and rebellion, which we regularly see in the life of Israel.[39] Second, in this new covenant, God writes his instruction on the heart—at the center of one's life.[40] Finally, the result is a community in which all know God (Jer 31:34).[41] As shown in Gentry and Wellum, other similarities and differences can be seen:

Similarity of the New Covenant to the Old Covenant

1. Basis is the same (the grace of God)
2. Purpose is the same (cf. 1 Pet. 2:9–10)
3. Initiated by blood (Heb. 9:6–10:18)
4. Character of divine instruction is the same (Rom. 13:8; Gal. 5:14)

Dissimilarity of the New Covenant to the Old Covenant

1. Better mediator (without sin)
2. Better sacrifice (Isa. 42:6; 52:13–53:12; Heb. 9:6–10:18)
3. Better provision (the Spirit of God, Ezek. 36:24–28)
4. Better promise (impartation of a new heart, Ezek. 36:24–28)[42]

[39] See Gentry and Wellum, 548.

[40] See Gentry and Wellum, 551–52.

[41] See Gentry and Wellum, 554.

[42] Taken from Gentry and Wellum, 563. Used by permission of Crossway, a publishing ministry of Good News Publishers, Wheaton, IL 60187, www.crossway.org.

The new covenant, then, is highlighted by God's promise to transform a people to be a true light of obedience to the nations so that, in turn, all could turn to him and be saved and renewed. This new covenant is greater because of Jesus Christ and the salvation he has secured.[43]

But to what degree has the new covenant arrived? The rest of the New Testament operates from a perspective called "inaugurated eschatology." This idea means that while certain aspects of the end times have started, believers wait for its fullness to come. The promises and hopes of the covenants have been fulfilled in Christ and have begun to be applied to the church, while the church waits for Christ's return, when those full benefits will be applied. This balance is important for Christians, who know that the source of their future hope, just as the source of their current blessings, is and always will be the triune God through Christ.

Conclusion

As we have seen, the covenants provide the plotline for all of Scripture, with a bit more detail and explanation than the simple creation-fall-redemption rubric. The covenants only make sense in light of that rubric, in light of God's quest to redeem a fallen world, but they highlight for us the way that God chose to do so: by calling one man, Abraham, and using his family to be a holy nation through which God himself would eventually come to reconcile the world. All of God's plan for reconciliation and redemption—not just for Israel but for all people and all of creation—comes

[43] See Gentry and Wellum, 731.

through these covenants.[44] A proper biblical ethics remains rooted in and responsible to this overarching plan, revealed in the Old and New Testaments.

---

[44] As we have seen, "Thus, through the covenants . . . God reveals how his image bearers ought to live and how he will establish his saving reign and restore creation through a promised, obedient Son." Gentry and Wellum, 653. Used by permission of Crossway, a publishing ministry of Good News Publishers, Wheaton, IL 60187, www.crossway.org.

4

Old and New Testament Ethics

How do we move from the biblical story, and the unity provided through the covenants, to an explanation of biblical ethics? This can happen in a variety of ways, some of which we will take up in our final chapter, "The Practice of Biblical Ethics." But we can begin here by connecting the overarching story and the covenants to some prominent Old Testament and New Testament texts and themes related to ethics. One road we will not take is the claim that the Bible simply does not contain many ethical texts.[1] Driving this sort of wedge into the Bible by relying on modern genre categories only obscures the ethical thread throughout the entire Bible.

As noted earlier, biblical ethics is not simply grabbing one verse, tearing it out of Scripture, and claiming that it "applies" to

[1] See, for example, Richard A. Burridge, "Imitating Mark's Jesus: Imagination, Scripture, and Inclusion in Biblical Ethics Today," *Sewanee Theological Review* 50, no. 1 (2006): 13.

a contemporary situation. At the same time, particular verses do matter and certainly do apply. But they apply through the biblical, covenantal context in which God spoke those particular words. Furthermore, many biblical texts contain ethics that are assumed indirectly or sometimes represented through the evaluation of actions.[2] This takes practice, which we will do in this chapter. First, we will approach a few key Old Testament texts that are often applied in Christian ethics. By situating these texts properly in their historical-redemptive context, we will articulate how it is that these texts come to inform and invite Christian obedience today. Second, we will look at common Old Testament ethical themes as well, seeking to better interpret and enhance these themes by properly connecting them to the story and the covenants. Third and fourth, we will follow the same pattern with common New Testament texts and themes.

We are not attempting here to explore every key text or every important theme in the Bible. Instead, we will select a few representative texts and themes to practice properly rooting them in the biblical, redemptive, covenantal context in a way that will make better sense of how they contribute to a consistent, unified voice of biblical ethics.

Key Texts in the Old Testament

The Ten Commandments

The Ten Commandments jump to mind almost immediately when we think about ethics in the Bible, and for good reason. There are

[2] See Ruben Zimmermann, "The 'Implicit Ethics' of New Testament Writings: A Draft on a New Methodology for Analyzing New Testament Ethics," *Neotestamenica* 43, no. 2 (2009): 399, https://www.jstor.org/stable/43048728.

several reasons for this, and some quite practical. For instance, we often find rules comforting; they are clear. Additionally, the Ten Commandments, while clearly applicable to the wandering Israelites, also apply to contemporary life with little need for imagination. It can be difficult to think about how to apply various laws in Leviticus; "honor your father and mother" at least seems more straightforward, even today.

Not only do the Ten Commandments seem easier to apply, but some scholars propose that the commandments be used as the general framework for biblical ethics. For instance, in *An Introduction to Biblical Ethics*, David Jones structures the entire book around the law. He divides the law into categories—ceremonial, civil, and moral, as has been common but controversial in Christian thinking—and argues that the moral law always reflects God's character and is therefore always binding.[3] The Ten Commandments, then, are viewed as the summary of the moral law and therefore uniquely and universally binding.

Two problems emerge from this interpretation. First, dividing the law into ceremonial, civil, and moral categories makes sense to modern sensibilities of categorization, but the Bible itself never makes these divisions, and in fact, such divisions emphasize difference over unity and fail to consider adequately the connections between the supposed "categories." For instance, wouldn't it make sense for God's character to underlie not only the moral law but the rest of it too? Second, the discussion of the law in the New Testament tends to revolve around images of the new covenant and sanctification, not with a framework centered on the Ten Commandments. While this approach to the Ten Commandments might be clear and

---

[3] See, for instance, Jones, *An Introduction to Biblical Ethics*, 57–60 (see chap. 1, n. 6).

useful for some modern Christian ethicists, it puts too much of a burden on this text, and it does so for the wrong reasons.

Before we get carried away, let me say clearly: the Ten Commandments are certainly important for biblical ethics. But how we describe that importance and how we relate the Ten Commandments to the Bible as a whole require a modified approach. Let's begin by situating the Ten Commandments in the biblical story and in God's promises, rather than seeking to abstract it and make it universal. In the book of Exodus, God has miraculously brought his people out of Egypt, just as he had promised he would. The exodus is rooted in God's promise to make Abraham the father of a great nation (Gen 12:2) and in the further specific promise that God would deliver Abraham's descendants from captivity (Genesis 15). God gave the Ten Commandments after delivering his people.

But how do the commandments function in connection with that promise? When we see God giving laws to his people in the Old Testament, we might sometimes think we have found a sort of bait-and-switch: "I'll deliver you, but then you'd better live up to all of these rules, some of which are rooted in my eternal character, and some of which are pretty arbitrary." That is not what is happening, though. This covenant had no stipulations; God gave it in the form of a suzerainty treaty, an ancient example not of something to be earned but reflecting an already established reality. This type of treaty served not to create a new relationship but to lay out what an existing relationship was to look like. The key clue is found in another piece of the promise that God made to Abraham.

God did not only promise that he would make Abraham's descendants a great nation, he also promised that this nation would have a special role to play. In Genesis 12 God speaks of the nation being a blessing, one through whom *all the nations of the earth would be blessed* (Gen 12:2–3). We can gloss over this too quickly when we (rightly) identify that the main way Israel would be a blessing would be through the ultimate incarnation, death, and resurrection of Jesus Christ. That is true, but the blessing is not limited to that.

God's commands to Israel are rooted in making them a blessing to all nations in two ways. First, their way of life distinguishes them from the pagan nations and demonstrates what human flourishing is supposed to look like when people live in relation to God. Second, their way of life was meant to preserve the family through which God had promised to bring Jesus. All of the Old Testament laws serve this purpose: who the people of God are to be so that they might be the blessing to the nations that God has already said he would make them.

Hosea 6:6

> "For I desire faithful love and not sacrifice,
> the knowledge of God rather than burnt offerings."

Understood in the right way, this verse opens for us a broad and helpful way of thinking about the laws in the Old Testament. God desires more from his people than mere adherence to laws—in this case, laws regarding sacrifices and burnt offerings. It seems that the people of God were attempting to check the boxes of the law, but God was not fooled because they were violating the underlying redemptive context of these laws, thus rendering them meaningless. God wanted faithful love, an idea moving beyond mere sentimentalism into adoration rooted in covenant faithfulness. When we place this key text into its proper context, we can better understand how it continues to call to us today. Just as God was not impressed with checking sacrifice boxes then, he is not impressed with checking rule boxes today. He desires deeper heart transformation, actions rooted in faithful love, not forced conformity alone.

At the same time, we must guard ourselves against turning verses like this into something God never intended by forcing an anemic, cultural definition of love into the beginning. God is not advocating some proto-situational ethics, claiming that the only way to determine the "right" is to determine what "love" would do in a particular situation. The term here is "faithful love," which reminds us that the love God desires is one rooted in his own example of covenant-keeping love.

When we consider this verse from both angles, we see how reading it properly within a larger biblical ethic protects us from two dangers: dead legalism and unrooted, standardless sentimentalism.

Micah 6:8

> Mankind, he has told each of you what is good
> and what it is the LORD requires of you:
> to act justly,
> to love faithfulness,
> and to walk humbly with your God.

This summary statement from the prophet Micah serves well to capture the heart of what sort of ethics God called his people to in the Old Testament. Similar to Hos 6:6, this verse emphasizes broader categories than simply following laws. Justice, faithfulness, humility: these virtues guide a life lived before God.

Some scholars see this verse playing a unique role in Christian morality. For instance, Gary Tyra uses it to frame all of ethics: "It's simply my contention that all the moral behaviors commended in the Scriptures can be accurately subsumed under the three categories of acting justly, loving with mercy and walking humbly/faithfully before God."[4] Tyra marshals two major arguments for this centrality: cardinal virtues have always been well-known to Christian ethics, and, more importantly for our consideration here, both the Old and New Testaments connect to these verses.[5] For the Old Testament, he cites Ps 35:5–6 and 89:14, as well as Hos 2:19–20. In the New Testament, Tyra notes the way that Jesus's teaching echoes these same three virtues in such places as Matt 23:23, which states, "Woe to you, scribes and Pharisees, hypocrites! You pay a tenth of mint, dill, and cumin, and yet you have neglected the more important matters of the law—justice, mercy, and faithfulness. These things should have been done without neglecting the others." Because of these connections, Tyra stands Mic 6:8 at the center of Christian moral faithfulness. Tyra is clearly onto something here, but he argues for it in a disjointed way, one that tends to chop up Scripture and highlight connections between the pieces ("this virtue pops up elsewhere") rather than demonstrating the consistency between Mic 6:8, the old covenant itself, and the promises of the new covenant.

When we place Mic 6:8 into the broader redemptive storyline of Scripture, we can better understand the warning it issues while also seeing how it draws God's people into a right relationship to ethics. First, the warning. Micah was writing to people who knew the law—some of whom may even have been good at following the letter of the law. This warning then, similar to

---

[4] Gary Tyra, *Pursuing Moral Faithfulness* (Downers Grove, IL: IVP Academic, 2015), 169.

[5] See Tyra, 170–75.

the warning in Hosea, is that it is possible for someone to check boxes, even for good reasons, and miss out on the ethical life with God that the Bible calls God's people toward. Second, we also see that God's law is aimed at something positive and deeper: virtues such as justice, faithfulness, and humility. We do not need to see these as opposing the law, as though Micah were saying, "Break the law, but do it with humility." Rather, these virtues serve to qualify and clarify what the law is pointing at and drawing people toward: a right relationship with God, one that renounces the sinful inheritance we have from Adam but one that does so in a deep and lasting way. Micah 6:8, in fact, is pointing at something other prophets point at as well: true life with God requires a deep transformation, a new heart to replace our "hearts of stone" (Ezek 36:26). Micah 6:8 only makes sense poised as Micah was within the old covenant but yearning for the transformation promised by the new covenant.

Key Themes in Old Testament Ethics

Understanding Old Testament ethics requires not only looking at key texts within the broader story but also putting the texts within Israel's worldview. In his work, Christopher J. H. Wright has provided helpful steps toward this goal. He emphasizes that the Israelite worldview provided answers to several key questions:

1. *Where are we?* We are part of a good creation that belongs to God.
2. *Who are we?* In the broad sense, we are humans made in the image of God. Specifically, Israel is the people of God.
3. *What's gone wrong?* Humans have rebelled against God, and this has brought consequences into all of life.

4. *What's the solution?* God addresses the problem by a project of redemption through his chosen people.[6]

We see here many of the elements of the overarching story (chapter 2), and the covenants and redemption (chapter 3) come into play to consider Old Testament ethics in a holistic way. As Wright puts it, "It is only within this matrix of assumptions that Old Testament ethics makes sense."[7] Further, a proper understanding of the overarching story beyond the Old Testament is necessary to understand how Old Testament ethics speaks consistently with overall biblical ethics.

Keeping this worldview in mind, we can also identify three angles for approaching biblical ethics in the Old Testament. Wright describes them this way: the theological angle (the LORD, the God of Israel), the social angle (Israel as the chosen people in a special relationship with God), and the economic angle (the land God has promised and given to Israel).[8] These angles do not so much summarize biblical ethics in the Old Testament as they provide vantage points from which to consider key elements. From the first angle we are reminded that all of ethics is theological; we cannot cordon off parts, making some about God and others just about practical matters, or something like that. Further, even individual laws focused on particular people cannot be interpreted properly outside of the social context of Israel as the people of God—which also reconnects us to the overarching story and the reminder that this people was chosen by God to be the people through whom he

---

[6] For these four questions and answers, see Wright, *Old Testament Ethics for the People of God*, 18 (see chap. 1, n. 3).

[7] Wright, 19.

[8] See Wright, 19.

would bless the world. Certainly, this task must be held close to our understanding of Israel's social context. Finally, the economic angle reminds us that matters related to the land and to flourishing within it are not secondary to biblical ethics but are necessarily included because of the types of promises God has made. Therefore, when we read about economic concerns in the Old Testament, we must remember that while they may have broader applicability, they are first and foremost relevant to the promises God made to Israel as his people, chosen to bring forth the Messiah, through whom the world could be saved.

With this framework in mind, filled out even further with our considerations of the extended biblical context covered in earlier chapters, we will consider some popular themes for Old Testament ethics and observe how they fit properly within a fuller biblical framework.

Persons and the Imago Dei

If you have heard someone talk about ethics by drawing on biblical texts, you have likely heard that one of the most important ways the Bible shapes our ethics is how it describes humans at creation. God created Adam and Eve—and nothing else—in his image (Gen 1:27). This detail is not a minor one. As we explored in chapter 2, Adam and Eve's creation in God's image—and the task that God gives them to serve as co-rulers, visually expanding his rule through the whole creation—sets up the story in a vital way. Oftentimes, however, when we highlight "human persons created in the image of God" for our ethical reflection, we are tempted to pull the notion completely out of the biblical narrative. So, "humans are created in the image of God" becomes a way to theologically ground something like "humans have value, and life should be respected." We might understand this logical move, and we might even need it, but it skips a few steps that a fully biblical ethics delivers.

When we isolate "created in God's image" from the story in which those created in God's image play a key part, we can end up with the value and dignity of human life without the connection to God considered at all. In other words, when we forget the broader storyline of biblical ethics, we might find ourselves stealing a concept—even a concept faithfully, though partially, understood—and putting it to work for our predetermined conclusions. Furthermore, we can locate ways that certain assumptions build on concepts such as this one, for what Zimmermann notes about the New Testament applies to the old as well: "Values in a text do not appear in isolation; rather they are used with argumentations, in comparison to other values or even in a hierarchy of values."[9]

Two main problems emerge from this reduction of "image of God" notions. First, the reduction can isolate individual persons from the communities in which they are formed and through which God works to transform them into the image of Christ. Individual ethics in the Bible is always community-shaped, especially in the Old Testament.[10] Certainly God calls individuals and provides laws for individuals; individuality is an aspect of what is going on in biblical ethics. But the focus on the individual created in the image of God can obscure the reality of how much of biblical ethics is community driven and community informed.

Second, this logic can encourage us to think of human life as valuable in and of itself, simply to be activated by an individual pursuing whatever it is they want to pursue. In other words,

---

[9] Zimmermann, "The 'Implicit Ethics' of New Testament Writings," 403.

[10] See Wright, *Old Testament Ethics for the People of God*, 363.

there are at least two key elements to the image of God: humans are made in the image of God, and that image includes (for some) or is applied to (for others) the task of ruling with God, extending his rule over all creation. Being created in the image of God means more than the value of individuals as individuals; it includes individuals living in connection to God in the people of God.

This is not to say that the doctrine of the image of God cannot be applied to notions of protecting the vulnerable. This concept drives Christian ethics to care about and value human life. But when we connect this theme to the broader biblical story, we see that those made in the image of God are valuable because God created us in his image and has called us to serve him.

Land

The Promised Land plays a key role in the Old Testament. God promised Abraham that he would make him into a nation and give that nation a place; much of the Old Testament revolves around God's people coming into that land, living within that land, being exiled from that land, and returning to it.

But how are we to interpret the land, the ethical issues related to the Promised Land in the Old Testament, and the impact on our own understanding of land? Wright notes three options for interpreting the land. First, the paradigmatic approach sees a reflection in God's relation to Israel in their land, a reflection meant to demonstrate truths about God's relation to all humankind on the earth.[11] Second, an eschatological approach builds on that idea that God's purposes with Israel will ultimately include all people and the

[11] See Wright, 182.

whole world, in a perfected, transformed, new creation.[12] As he puts it, "The historical people and land were part of the *process* of God's redemptive purpose, not its final, perfected *product*."[13] Finally, a typological approach refracts the notion of the land through the prism of the Messiah, seeing even the land promises fulfilled and expanded in Christ. Wright explains this well:

> To be *in Christ*, just as to be *in the land*, denotes first, a status and a relationship that have been *given* by God; second, a position of inclusion and security in God's family; and third, a commitment to live worthily by fulfilling the practical responsibilities towards those who share the same relationship with you. This is what is meant by the *typological* understanding of the significance of Israel's land. It simply means treating the land as we do other great features and themes of the Old Testament, by relating it to the person and work of the Messiah, and through him to the nature of the community of those "in Christ," messianic Israel.[14]

Understood rightly, each of these approaches lends insight to biblical ethics. The typological approach tells us that the land can be fulfilled in Christ while also still communicating true eschatological elements. It also connects us to God's relationship to all humankind because both eschatology and God's relationship to people are rooted in the Messiah.

One caution emerges, however. If we read about the Promised Land in the Old Testament without any of these paradigms, we can make the mistake of oversimplification. To say something

---

[12] See Wright, 184.

[13] Wright, 185.

[14] Wright, 192.

like, "God cares about the land in the Old Testament; therefore, we should care about the environment and agree with this policy" irons out the redemptive canonical framework that is necessary for faithfully understanding this theme.[15] It is not that our environmental ethics today can ignore the land promises and land stewardship in the Old Testament; rather, we must refract the land theme through Christ in order to understand it fully. We will return to this notion in our next chapter.

Justice

Justice is one of the most important obviously ethical themes in the Old Testament, one that can easily be co-opted into agendas and stories that ignore the broader biblical context. In Wright's work, he helpfully reminds us that justice is something God cares about and that only God can ultimately bring: "If it was unthinkable that the Judge of all the earth should not do right, how much more unthinkable was it that this same God should not eventually intervene to judge the accumulated wrongs of humanity and put things right once and for all. Only God can finally 'get things sorted'. Only God *can*, but God assuredly *will*, is the unshakeable affirmation

---

[15] A sophisticated example of this approach can be found in Ellen Davis, *Scripture, Culture, and Agriculture: An Agrarian Reading of the Bible* (New York: Cambridge University Press, 2009). Davis provides a robust analysis of Old Testament texts and brings them into dialogue with contemporary concerns, but she pays too little attention to the typological elements. It is not that these texts *do not* apply to how we think about agrarianism or land use but that the way they do apply to those issues cannot be understood fully without being connected to the whole picture of faith and life provided in biblical ethics, rooted in Christ.

of many Old Testament texts."[16] This insistence that "God will" reminds us that isolated verses about justice in the Old Testament are not the whole story. Any treatment of the theme of justice in biblical ethics must center on the cross of Christ, where God most clearly displayed his character and commitment to justice. Justice was important in Israel not only because God is a just God but because part of the reason God called and chose Israel was to display a light to the nations. Justice is always theological. Injustice is inconsistent with God's character; if Israel tolerates injustice, they are lying about God.

Cries for justice abound today. These cries are important, for God is a God of justice. It is still a theological issue. But when we approach justice divorced from the cross, apart from God's own actions for and plans for ultimate justice, we make justice itself a god. For instance, sometimes we can disconnect justice from God's plan for all and emphasize justice only for certain groups. As one scholar puts it, "Biblical justice is biased in favor of the poor and the weak of the earth."[17] The problem with statements like this is that they lack the detail and logic that connects the partial truth of the statement to the ultimate truth. God cares about the oppressed because he cares about justice, and they are not experiencing it. It is not that biblical justice is biased but that biblical justice addresses injustice. To claim bias for certain groups can end up cultivating new forms of injustice.

It is not that justice does not matter or that justice does not have social implications. It does. But justice is ultimately theological,

---

[16] Wright, *Old Testament Ethics for the People of God*, 278.

[17] Stephen Charles Mott, *Biblical Ethics and Social Change*, 2nd ed. (New York: Oxford University Press, 2011), 59.

achieved only by God's work in Christ and the church—and ultimately in the return of Christ. As Christians today advocate for justice, we must continually remember the function of justice—pointing to God's good character and pointing forward to God's already-but-not-yet-here kingdom.

Holiness

We cannot properly understand the notion of justice when we remove it from the biblical narrative, because justice is rooted in God's holiness. As Wright puts it, "It is clear that for Israel the whole idea of justice was wrapped up with the qualities and characteristics of the Lord, their God, and especially connected to the covenant relationship between Israel and the Lord. Justice is essentially relational and covenantal."[18] Justice makes no sense apart from the character of God and the covenants he has made.

Since justice must be rooted in the story of the Bible, and God—who is holy—is the main character of that story, we cannot have justice without holiness. This fact is what leads some ethicists, such as Scott Rae, to argue that "the central concept that unifies Old Testament ethics is holiness."[19] We do not identify holiness simply by identifying the right decision to make in particular ethical crises; rather, holiness is a character trait that God works in his people through the Holy Spirit, a character trait that we should carry into decision making. The fact that God calls us to be holy (see, for instance, Exod 19:6; Lev 19:2; 20:7, 26; 21:8; 1 Thess 4:7; 1 Pet 1:16) is one of the best rationales for Christian interest in

---

[18] Wright, *Old Testament Ethics for the People of God*, 258–59.

[19] Rae, *Moral Choices*, 76 (see chap. 1, n. 11).

virtue ethics—we are not called only to do our duty or to maximize the good or any of the other moral calculations on offer.[20] Rather, we are to be people of a certain character, one that only God can ultimately bestow. (And our need for God to work in us is a key corrective to secular virtue theory. Some Christian accounts of virtue ethics make the same mistake—leaning too heavily on the work that we do rather than on the work that God does.)

While God's holiness is not something we can achieve, it is something to which he calls us. When we locate this idea in the proper place in the story of the Bible, we see that the holiness of God's people is part of how Israel and the church are lights that shine to the world; holiness is part of the way the church bears witness to the truth of the gospel and the reality of God's kingdom. Even if holiness unifies Old Testament ethics, it only makes sense in light of the entire biblical narrative.

Key Texts in the New Testament

Christian ethics often draws on a myriad of texts in the New Testament to help us understand ethics. However, we often pluck these verses out of the broader story they are a part of, and in doing so we miss some of the deeper connections, motivations, and explanations. In what follows, we are going to process through several examples of texts, highlighting ways that approaching biblical ethics with an expectation of a unified voice can help us hear and see more of what God reveals and its impact on ethics.

---

[20] For one example of using virtue ethics to ground biblical ethics, see Kyle Fedler, *Exploring Christian Ethics: Biblical Foundations for Morality* (Louisville: Westminster John Knox, 2006).

Matthew 28:19–20

"Go, therefore, and make disciples of all nations, baptizing them in the name of the Father and of the Son and of the Holy Spirit, teaching them to observe everything I have commanded you. And remember, I am with you always, to the end of the age."

The Great Commission identifies evangelism as a key priority of Christians, but in it Jesus describes evangelism in a way that draws biblical ethics close to it. Verse 20 makes it clear that part of the task is "teaching them to observe everything I have commanded you." Locating this passage within its canonical redemptive context helps us notice three truths.

First, the message of the gospel ties directly into right living. Grammatically speaking, the "teaching" is expanding on "make disciples," not adding optional detail. The idea that the Bible does not have a consistent ethic or that ethical issues are minor issues in comparison to the "big-picture agreement" around the gospel does not fit with this basic statement that Jesus makes.

Second, Jesus did not shy away from the language of "commands." While the New Testament certainly identifies virtues (or, more precisely, fruits of the Spirit), Jesus still uses the language of "commands" here. If biblical ethics backs away from actual commands, making the faithful life of the Christian something vague and self-determined, it fails to obey Christ here.

Third, biblical ethics is something that can (and must) be taught. Ancient traditions such as virtue ethics emphasized that becoming a virtuous person happens through practice. Do just acts; become a just person. While Christianity certainly identifies faithful practices, Jesus did not go so far as to say that "ethics is only something you can learn through practice." He expected his followers to teach obedience, to teach ethics, as part of basic discipleship from the place of a transformed heart.

Romans 8:29

"For those he foreknew he also predestined to be conformed to the image of his Son, so that he would be the firstborn among many brothers and sisters."

This verse shapes biblical ethics in several ways. First, we learn that believers are going to be conformed to the image of Jesus—this is not an optional add-on for some believers but not others. In fact, it is an expansion and fulfillment of our being created in the image of God, for Jesus is the true image of God. Reading this verse on the individual level, we are reminded that sanctification is part of God's plan for every follower of Jesus, even if that sanctification takes different paces and paths with some than others. There is still a clear goal: the image of Christ. Questions of ethics, then, are not left up to individuals to determine what might be best; rather, Jesus's image is the standard. The task of ethics, when rooted in sanctification, is to wrestle through what course of action is most fitting with the image of the Son.

This verse reminds us of something deeper as well. Paul was writing to Roman Christians, laying out for them what it means to be the church in the time between Jesus's ascension and return. He had a lot to say about what they were to believe, but in places like this he reminds God's people that their focus is not only on right belief (though of course not less); additionally, part of being the church is being instrumental in this sanctification. In other words, Paul was not only encouraging individuals here; he was also giving to a body of believers a sense of what the Christian life is about. The church should be concerned with ethics because it is a non-negotiable part of Rom 8:29, which tells us what God is doing in individual lives but also in the church as a whole (and through the church's work too).

Galatians 5:22–24 (and the Beatitudes)

"But the fruit of the Spirit is love, joy, peace, patience, kindness, goodness, faithfulness, gentleness, and self-control. The law is not against such things. Now those who belong to Christ Jesus have crucified the flesh with its passions and desires."

These verses express the work of sanctification in the life of the believer. The Holy Spirit produces fruit, and belonging to Christ also means separation from worldly passions and desires. This passage connects back to another significant passage for ethics in the New Testament: the Sermon on the Mount and, more specifically, the Beatitudes. Like the fruit of the Spirit in Galatians, Jesus's words in the Beatitudes and the Sermon on the Mount as a whole expound the character of the Christian life.

Sometimes such passages are swept up into a narrative about Christians developing virtue in the Christian life, and rightly so. But as we discussed earlier in this chapter with regard to holiness, we must be careful about how the Bible clearly distinguishes the fruit of the Spirit and the holiness God expects from the virtues as expounded in the Greek philosophical tradition. According to the Bible these are the *fruit of the Spirit*, not the fruit of habit formation or the well-earned attitude of the devoted few. (Granted, the Holy Spirit works in and through us, including work we may experience as our own, even in doing things like developing habits toward virtue.) But when we too quickly identify language like this with the virtue tradition, we rip this verse out of the biblical story, too often forgetting that this is work that God has promised to complete through the Holy Spirit.

Ephesians 4:20–24

"But that is not how you came to know Christ, assuming you heard about him and were taught by him, as the truth is in Jesus, to take off your former way of life, the old self that is corrupted by deceitful desires, to be renewed in the spirit of your minds, and to put on the new self, the one created according to God's likeness in righteousness and purity of the truth."

In this passage written to the church at Ephesus, Paul provided a framework for thinking about holy living as a result of sanctification. Believers are to "take off" their former ways of living, be spiritually renewed, and "put on" a new self, which is described as righteous and pure.

We could draw many elements out of this passage, but one particular piece is clear here that is very muddy in the world around us: desires can be deceitful. Such desires corrupt the old self. Worldly approaches to human life seldom admit this and instead insist that "authenticity" means acknowledging one's desires, being positive about them rather than ashamed of them, and pursuing those desires. Many people want to put such attitudes under the notion of "autonomy," ripped from any context but expressive individualism. Such pursuit is simply pursuing lies, as Paul pointed out here.

Often, however, Christians are not much better. We do not recognize the seriousness that Paul highlighted here; we are tempted to downplay just how deceived we can be. Further, many approaches to ethics in Christian circles can emphasize the right or wrong thing to do, without even engaging in talk about the level of deceitful desires. Here we see why a unified biblical ethic is required. It helps us see a fuller picture of the human struggle and the only solution, and it also drives us again and again to the character and works of God, who is the one who grounds righteousness and truth in this passage, the "antidote" to our deceitful desires.

Colossians 3:5–10

"Therefore, put to death what belongs to your earthly nature: sexual immorality, impurity, lust, evil desire, and greed, which is idolatry. Because of these, God's wrath is coming upon the disobedient, and you once walked in these things when you were living in them. But now, put away all the following: anger, wrath, malice, slander, and filthy language from your mouth. Do not lie to one another, since you have put off the old self with its practices and have put on the new self. You are being renewed in knowledge according to the image of your Creator."

In this passage, Paul gave specific insight into what the Christian life should not include. Each of these specific sins falls clearly outside the bounds of biblical ethics, but this passage is more than simply a list of sins to avoid or repent of. How do Paul's words connect with the broader biblical story?

First, note the violent imagery used: "put to death" the earthly, sinful nature. Paul made clear that this is no easy task, nor is it one to take lightly. By phrasing it this way, Paul also connected with the broader idea of sanctification in the New Testament. He was not telling the Colossians to earn their salvation but rather insisting that their salvation must and will be worked out in their lives. It will not be easy; it is not just about a list of sins to avoid but about putting to death our old nature.

Second, Paul still mentioned specific sins, practices that are out of bounds. But he did so in a way that is not quite the same as the law in the Old Testament, or a new law for Christians. He wrote in the imperative; he commanded his readers. But he rooted the command not in achieving compliance to a law but in living according to a new, redeemed, reborn nature. Informed by the biblical story, this passage resists creating new laws, but it also insists that the Christian life is a life of holy living and growth.

1 Peter 2:22–24

"He did not commit sin, and no deceit was found in his mouth; when he was insulted, he did not insult in return; when he suffered, he did not threaten but entrusted himself to the one who judges justly. He himself bore our sins in his body on the tree; so that, having died to sins, we might live for righteousness. By his wounds you have been healed."

In these verses, Peter provided us with a succinct reminder of the place of ethics in a Christian life informed by the entire trajectory of the Bible. In verse 24, we see a clear purpose statement, one that tells us why Jesus died for our sins: so that we might live righteously.

Placing this verse within the broader biblical storyline helps us see how righteous living lines up with the other parts. As we have seen, God's project of redemption started right after sin entered the world. Sometimes we can be tempted to think of redemption as merely saving us from the penalty we deserve. It is surely that, but Peter made clear that it is more. We are redeemed to be reunited with God, to live in relationship with him as we were always intended to do. The life lived in relationship with God is a life of righteousness.

This informs the way we approach biblical ethics because it reminds us that biblical ethics is not about proof texting certain sins or certain right actions; rather, the Bible's unified voice on ethics shapes our sense of what righteousness is, that we might live for righteousness.

Key Themes in New Testament Ethics

Focal Images: Community, Cross, New Creation

In his monumental work on New Testament ethics, Richard Hays argues that three focal images help us with ethical interpretation in the New Testament. The text's unity, he says, revolves around a single fundamental story, which he summarizes as: "The God of Israel, the creator of the world, has acted (astoundingly) to rescue a lost and broken world through the death and resurrection of Jesus; the full scope of that rescue is not yet apparent, but God has created a community of witnesses to this good news, the church. While awaiting the grand conclusion of the story, the church, empowered by the Holy Spirit, is called to reenact the loving obedience of Jesus Christ and thus to serve as a sign of God's redemptive purposes for the world."[21] This summary echoes the story we covered earlier in this book. Perhaps Hays's focal images can give us additional insight into seeing not only the New Testament's single ethical voice but the entire Bible's—in fact, God's voice.

If we look closely, we will see Hays's focal images in his summary. The first is community, which he mentions in the above summary as "a community of witnesses to this good news." As he puts it, "The church is a countercultural community of discipleship, and

[21] Hays, *The Moral Vision of the New Testament*, 193 (see chap. 1, n. 4).

this community is the primary addressee of God's imperatives. . . . Thus, the primary sphere of moral concern is not the character of the individual but the corporate obedience of the church."[22] Second is the cross. Faithfulness to God in this world follows the paradigm of the cross, and "the community as a whole is called to follow in the way of Jesus' suffering."[23] Hays's third focal image, new creation, connects to and extends the community and cross images: "The church embodies the power of the resurrection in the midst of a not-yet-redeemed world."[24] For Hays, each of these focal images comes from the texts themselves but also serves as a helpful way to draw out key ethical dimensions of individual texts.

Hays situates the images in a certain way. He insists that finding unity requires "metaphorical imagination" that can focus the diverse contents of various texts.[25] Not just any image will do this work; instead, images should arise from the texts themselves.[26] Additionally, these "images would simultaneously summarize the story told in (or presupposed by) Scripture and govern the interpretation of individual texts by placing them within a coherent narrative framework."[27] Finally, there are three main criteria for such images: a textual basis, no serious tension with major emphases in the New Testament, and ability to highlight central ethical concerns.[28] These focal images, he suggests, seem to fit this bill.

While these focal images help make sense of New Testament ethics in one way, they are limited in other ways. First of all,

---

[22] Hays, 196.
[23] Hays, 197.
[24] Hays, 198.
[25] Hays, 194.
[26] See Hays, 194.
[27] Hays, 195.
[28] See Hays, 195.

Hays's "community" focal image overplays the notion of corporate obedience by playing it off of individual character. How can the community obey God if not by collectively obeying God as individuals? There is a virtuous circularity here, as community forms individuals and individuals make up communities, but Hays's way of stating it drives a wedge in the middle of this circle and overemphasizes the community in a way that downplays individual obedience. Second, Hays makes both the suffering of Christ and the resurrection of Christ normative in similar ways without adequately recognizing the tension between the two. On one hand, why does Christ's suffering once-for-all on the cross mean that the church must also suffer? On the other hand, how does "embodying the power of the resurrection" fit with "suffering"? The answer lies not in identifying a different focal image but in recognizing that we need more than just the New Testament to make sense of even these images: we need a unified biblical story that centers on and culminates in the cross but leads forward to resurrection and eternal life with God. Hays's work helps us get a start in noticing consistency and unity in the New Testament's ethical witness, and these focal images can be useful in limited ways, especially if we are disciplined enough to connect the images into the overarching biblical story.

Love

"Love" is a popular center for ethics in the New Testament. On one hand, it seems obvious: from "love your neighbor as yourself" to "God is love," it seems that love works as a key theme. However, there are limitations to this position. We will start with some that Hays notes. Hays recognizes the limitations of love as an overarching theme. First, many New Testament writers do not focus on love as a central idea.[29] For instance, the book of Acts does not even use the word as a noun or a verb.[30] Second, love might be a theme in some books, but it is not an image. It is an interpretation of the image of the cross; we cannot understand love outside of that image.[31] Third, Hays writes that "love covers a multitude of sins in more ways than one."[32] By this he means that many times biblical scholars, theologians, and ethicists will use "love" to cover assertions of ethical relativism.[33] As he reminds us, "We can recover the power of love only by insisting that love's meaning is to be discovered in the New Testament's story of Jesus—therefore, in the cross."[34] Indeed!

We can extend Hays's critique of love as an overarching theme. Not only do we need the cross to understand love; we need the entire biblical story to understand properly the cross. In other words, we see something here that we saw with the focal images Hays does advocate: we not only need overarching ideas and images that help us interpret the individual texts, we also need to acknowledge that these ideas and images only make sense in light of the unified voice of the entire Bible. Using "love" can lead us to downplay or miss things when love is not bounded by the cross and the entire story of redemption.

Therefore, while love is certainly a key idea in the New Testament, and it certainly impacts the ethics of the New Testament, proposing it as a central theme can lead to a misunderstanding and misapplication. "Love" can be used to downplay aspects of the text,

---

[29] See Hays, 200.

[30] See Hays, 201.

[31] See Hays, 202.

[32] Hays, 202.

[33] Hays, 202.

[34] Hays, 202.

especially when we come to the Bible with our own definitions of love and insist that the Bible meet them.

Conclusion

The goal here was not to explore every relevant text in the Bible or the main themes related to ethics in the Old and New Testaments. Instead, we have covered some key ground and demonstrated how each of these texts and each of these themes only make sense when located within the broader witness of God across the entire Bible, as God works to redeem a people for himself. In doing so, he speaks with a unified voice, one that forms and transforms Christian ethics. Every text in the Bible matters: "every canonical and thus, for the community of faith normative text, can be read as an 'ethical text.'"[35] As N. T. Wright expounds with his notion of the "virtuous circle," each text of Scripture is drawn up into the way God uses not only his word but also the stories, examples, and practices of the faith community to form and shape his people.[36] Next, we will expand some of the main ways a whole-Bible biblical ethics emerges from Scripture.

[35] Zimmermann, "'Implicit Ethics' of New Testament Writings," 417.

[36] See chapter 8 in N. T. Wright, *After You Believe: Why Christian Character Matters* (New York: HarperCollins, 2010).

5

A Whole-Bible Biblical Ethics

As we have explored, the entire Bible hangs together with a consistent narrative about God's redemption of a people for himself, as his consistent character and steadfast love shine through various covenants culminating in Jesus Christ. When we think about biblical ethics, though, we often think of particular passages. These passages can be helpful but also at least slightly misunderstood and misapplied when we miss the way they contribute to God's unified plan and speak with a unified voice. Throughout the church's history, "Christians have looked to the Bible for theological concepts by which to understand their moral obligations, commandments by which to live, values by which to order personal and social existence, patterns of life worthy of emulation, and insight into the dynamics of character formation."[1] But looking to the Bible does not always yield easy answers.

Part of this challenge emerges from how we see great diversity within the Bible, especially with regard to ethical questions. As Allen Verhey reminds us, "Ethics in Scripture are diverse, not monolithic. Yet, the one God of Scripture still calls in it and through it for a faithful response, still forms and reforms conduct and character and community until they are something 'new,' something 'worthy of the gospel of Christ.'"[2] For some scholars, such as Verhey, we can deal with this problem by shifting our expectations a little, looking for something different than a moral code. For instance, the Gospel of Mark does not put forward a clear moral code, but it does encourage a moral posture that is far more demanding than a code.[3] Is this the answer to the problem: shifting our expectations a bit, emphasizing posture rather than proposals?

In short, no, for a few reasons. First, what logic determines whether something leads to a moral code or a moral posture? Does this shift occur merely because the text is old, because we cannot find the consistency, or because we cannot imagine how it would fit in our modern times? Such a shift might actually make it that much more difficult for an ancient text to speak prophetically to us today. We would be likely to silence the very aspects we most need. Second, moving through the Bible making these decisions would break up the text into separate and potentially competing "postures." Third, taking this approach abandons the actual key to understanding biblical ethics.

---

[1] Cosgrove, "Scripture in Ethics," in *Dictionary of Scripture and Ethics*, 13 (see chap. 1, n. 49).

[2] Verhey, "Ethics in Scripture," 11 (see chap. 1, n. 9).

[3] See Verhey, 8.

The key to hearing the Bible's unified voice is Jesus Christ. This truth applies to biblical theology—seeking to understand the Bible's unified revelation on particular theological topics—and also to biblical ethics. In particular, Jesus's sacrifice on the cross and the salvation accomplished there helps us interpret and apply everything that comes before it and everything that comes after it.

Others have acknowledged Jesus as the key to understanding biblical ethics, especially New Testament ethics. However, some examples of this focus do not quite cover this notion of Jesus as the key for biblical ethics. For instance, Richard Burridge writes the following:

> The biographical genre of the canonical gospels redirects our gaze back to begin with the historical Jesus, and in particular to a stress upon both his deeds and his words, his activities as well as his teachings. Furthermore, although the apostle Paul is writing letters in the genre of epistles, he also presumes an underlying narrative about the entire event of Jesus' life, death and resurrection. Finally, Paul and the writers of the gospels derive both from the Jewish tradition of *ma'aseh*, or precedent, and from the Graeco-Roman habit of *mimesis*, an insistence upon the imitation of Jesus through a narrative of his words and deeds as the way to lead a moral life or reflect upon ethical issues.[4]

The problem with a stance like this is not that it makes Jesus the center but that it shortens the narrative. A whole-Bible ethics centers on the narrative of the entire Bible. This narrative centers on and climaxes in the life, death, burial, and resurrection of Jesus. However, approaches like Burridge's can read the narrative of Jesus's

---

[4] Richard A. Burridge, *Imitating Jesus: An Inclusive Approach to New Testament Ethics* (Grand Rapids: Eerdmans, 2007), 4.

life outside the broader redemptive story context. Yes, the Gospels are narratives. But they themselves are always part of an extended narrative of redemption. We must keep this extended narrative in mind, centered on and made sense of in Christ alone. In this chapter, we will see how the biblical narrative, understood in this way, deals with various challenges, false solutions, and supposed "tensions" between the Old and New Testaments.

The Narrative of the Bible, Ethical Challenges, and Ethical Responses

One of the problems with our ability to understand biblical ethics is our tendency to come to the Bible with ethical questions and quandaries, searching for quick answers, and then leaving quickly if we find something useful, or slowly and disappointed if we do not. If the narrative of the Bible informs the unified voice of biblical ethics as I have argued, then biblical ethics cannot be a quandary-based ethics or an ethics that only responds to challenges when they arise.

First, this means that biblical ethics requires believers to immerse ourselves systematically in the text of Scripture. We will deal with this in more detail later, but it is worth mentioning now because it is vital to understanding how a whole-Bible biblical ethics emerges. We cannot simply proof text ethical positions, because in doing so we weaken what important verses are actually saying and pointing to. We also do not simply imitate what we find God doing, which leads to various problems.[5] Instead, we recognize that, as Douglas Sean O'Donnell and Leland Ryken have recently put it,

---

[5] For one perspective on potential problems, see Walter J. Houston, "The Character of YHWH and the Ethics of the Old Testament: Is *Imitatio Dei* Appropriate?" *Journal of Theological Studies* 58, no. 1 (2007): 1–25.

"throughout the Bible, meaning is communicated in various literary forms."[6] If we miss the way the Bible communicates meaning, we will miss (and misapply) the meaning. And that is true not only on the individual genre level.

Second, this means that we must grasp every text not only in its immediate literary context but within the broader biblical narrative. This practice will help us not misunderstand a particular command, who the command is for, or what it is intended to accomplish. This question of context leads us to an important caution and distinction, because "context" can be used in problematic ways.

Oliver O'Donovan gets at the root of the issue when he attempts to provide ways to better interpret individual biblical commands. He is worth quoting at length:

> It would certainly make life simpler if we could decide, either, with the existentialists, that the Bible contains no universalizable commands, or, with the rationalists of a previous age, that it contains nothing else. But since common-sense repudiates these simplicities, we are driven to seek criteria for dividing the one class of command from the other. Such criteria are to be found only in the context which makes the prescription intelligible. The particular command is justified in terms of the particular goal at which it aims or the particular situation which makes it appropriate: "Go from your country and your kindred to the land that I will show you . . . And I will make of you a great nation." The universalizable command is justified by reference to a universal principle, whether normative or descriptive: "My son, do

[6] Douglas Sean O'Donnell and Leland Ryken, *The Beauty and Power of Biblical Exposition: Preaching the Literary Artistry and Genres of the Bible* (Wheaton, IL: Crossway, 2022), 18.

> not despise the Lord's discipline or be weary of his reproof, for the Lord reproves him whom he loves . . ." Certainly there are cases in which a command appears with no justification attached at all; there are also cases in which the justification is an unexpected one, such as when the sabbath command is justified by reference to the Exodus. But it is no part of our contention that the exegesis of any text must always be straightforward, only that the canons governing it are clear: we can know at least what evidence we are looking for, even if it is not always easy to find.[7]

O'Donovan reminds us that while these sorts of connections are not necessarily easy to find, it does not follow that they are not there or that they are not worth finding.

We can press O'Donovan further here because even language like "universalizable" can move us away from the biblical narrative in an unhelpful way. If the story of God's redemption is truly the overarching story for all of humanity, then that story is "universalizable." But sometimes when people hear that term, they think of it as abstracted from any particular story or context. The task of biblical ethics is not to get away from the Bible's story but to rightly find ourselves in it. Anything that is "universalizable" is universal in this sense: it makes sense of the story that we are in, that we hear God within, and that we obey God in. Everything in the Bible is part of this narrative and therefore can be made sense of in this way. This does not mean we "universalize" something by taking it out of the story, but we universalize it by keeping the particular law (and ourselves) rooted within this universal story.

---

[7] Oliver O'Donovan, "Towards an Interpretation of Biblical Ethics," *Tyndale Bulletin* 27 (1976): 62–63.

When we consider an Old Testament law, for instance, we have to recognize that the Old Testament law as a whole operated as part of God's eternal plan focusing on Christ. Say, for instance, a law about not cooking a young goat in its mother's milk (Exod 23:19). We might be quick to set such a command aside, thinking that it has nothing to say to us because we are not subject to Old Testament dietary laws. (Here we might find ourselves guilty of imposing a foreign paradigm on the text in order to evade it.) While that would not be entirely off base (Christ frees us from the burden of the law), it misses something important about even this law. Part of what God was doing with his people Israel was using them to bring about his promises made to the whole world, to provide redemption. Therefore, laws related to Israel being distinct from its neighbors always served the purpose of keeping Israel distinct in order to display God's holiness and to preserve the line through which God would send the Messiah. In turn, then, this law reminds us of the church's role to be a visible community exemplifying the reality of the inbreaking kingdom of God, a display to the world around us. Christ as the key to even a law like this opens up biblical ethics in a more holistic manner.

The Part and the Whole

At my university, I often hear Bible professors talking about promising ways to engage undergraduate students. Studying the Bible in an academic context can be a challenging experience, for a variety of reasons. One colleague would frequently repeat his favorite phrase from teaching the Bible for nearly thirty years: "Context is king!" A catchy phrase for an important, foundational concept for interpreting anything. When it comes to biblical ethics, "context is king" comes into play somewhat frequently when scholars engage the biblical text, as it should. Sometimes, the historical context of the ancient world can help us better understand commands or prohibitions that make little sense to us. As far as this goes, understanding context is quite helpful.

But "context is king" is not always such an aid to understanding what the Bible actually teaches. Sometimes it serves as a diversion, one that can invert the text. One example of this has become quite common. It relates to the Bible's witness regarding human sexuality. The "context is king" argument in this case runs something like this: "Sure, the Bible says things about homosexuality. But in that context, homosexuality was not really like what it is in our contemporary society. If you read that in its context, you realize it has nothing to do with ours." While I am simplifying a bit, this argument is common, modified in various ways for different issues.

Another example emerges in relation to violence in the Bible. T. M. Lemos uses the symbol of the bow in the ancient Near East to unlock how the Old Testament applies to contemporary gun ownership. In short, Lemos makes the background context overdeterminative, importing symbolism and moral judgment into the text simply by the presence of the "bow." For Lemos, "While the use of the bow was not solely responsible for the presence or frequency of dehumanizing violence in ancient West Asia, it does seem that the bow had a role to play in the perpetuation and widespread nature of the violence-animalization-hypermasculinity complex that is domination personhood, when we consider the symbolic prominence of the bow and the dehumanizing violence associated with it."[8] Later, he makes a simple connection: "The symbolic similarity between the gun and the bow matters for Christians."[9]

---

[8] T. M. Lemos, "Israelite Bows and American Guns," in *God and Guns: The Bible against American Gun Culture*, ed. Christopher B. Hays and C. L. Crouch (Louisville: Westminster John Knox, 2022), 84.

[9] Lemos, "Israelite Bows and American Guns," 87.

According to Lemos, the bow was all about hypermasculinity, and guns are enough like bows that Christians must interpret the Bible to be against guns. I'm less interested here in the merits of gun ownership than I am in the way the cultural context plays such a large role, pushing the interpretation in a fanciful way that the author makes binding on all Christians. This imagery of the bow might inform interpretation, but here it drives interpretation beyond what the biblical text actually says—as evidenced by the fact that the author stipulates his interpretation not on the basis of biblical texts but on the basis of historical context primarily. Of course, this "context is king" mantra gets some important things right, but it also tempts us to believe that the context is *the* real key, the thing that not only unlocks meaning but that can help us wiggle away from the plain meaning of the Bible, right when it grabs us.

Perhaps a different phrase would be helpful: interpret the part in relation to the whole. This idea reminds us that any part of the Bible must not only be understood in its "context," it also reminds us of something about the larger context—the Bible is a unified book, a whole that gives sense to its various parts. When we approach issues of human sexuality from this vantage point, we recognize a few realities. First, while the ancient culture can help us understand something about the particular sins and struggles of that time, the whole testimony of Scripture still points clearly to the brokenness of sin. In other words, rather than using ancient cultural knowledge to claim a moral exception for our culture, we should expect to find new examples of brokenness and sin in our age, not examples that somehow escape the stain of sin and the resulting alienation from God. Our sins today might not correspond exactly to the sins the Bible critiques, but that does not mean they are virtues! Second, the Bible's narrative reminds us that the only hope of redemption is Christ's sacrificial death and the

Holy Spirit's sanctification of our hearts into the image of Christ who is the holiness of God. We do not redefine holiness; we trust Christ and plead with God to make us new.

We can see this principle at work with a less controversial example. In his work on biblical ethics, Oliver O'Donovan points briefly to God's command to Abraham to "go out" from his country (Gen 12:1). He notes, for instance, that the writer to the Hebrews clearly cares about this command because it serves as the condition for Abraham's faithful obedience, but there is no question to that author as to whether we are today called to "go out." O'Donovan explains that this command is "non-universalizable," because it was particular and addressed to a particular person at a particular point in time.[10] Yet we recognize that this text does in fact bring ethical impact—it serves as a great example of obedience later in Scripture. To extend O'Donovan's point, we might say that when we interpret this part of the story in light of the whole, we realize that it is not simply that this particular command cannot be made "universal" but that it is a concrete example of the universal call to obedience, and an example that makes sense in this pivotal point in God's redemptive work. We are not Abraham, but we are called to obey. The command still bears on us, but in a different way when we understand the whole picture. As part of God's people today, we are still called to radical obedience.

"The part and the whole" does not allow us to ignore context, or historical factors that can help us understand the Bible, but it does provide a proper priority and order to the interpretation. When we learn something about the historical situation, we bring that part to the whole story as well. Oftentimes, those who want to emphasize historical context seek to argue in a way that makes it

---

[10] O'Donovan, "Towards an Interpretation of Biblical Ethics," 68–69.

seem like because of the one detail they have discovered about the historical context, the text under consideration can be completely removed from the broader story. They insist, "The passage cannot mean *that*," when in reality the historical context can inform the whole narrative without radically changing the narrative. Listening for the Bible's unified voice—God's single, consistent voice—means connecting the pieces, understanding individual verses with obvious ethical import in light of the broader whole of the text and the redemptive story it is telling (and calling us into).

Conclusion

Whole-Bible ethics is not stringing biblical texts together. Instead, this approach insists on listening for the unified voice of God. Emphasizing this unified voice of Scripture, as we have done so far, can seem to fail to account for diversity within the Bible. Some might claim challenges or "contradictions" in the text, or at the very least "tensions." How does a whole-Bible approach help us navigate these tensions? We will turn to this topic next.

6

Challenges to Biblical Ethics

Modern biblical study has resisted moving from the Bible to normative ethics, to what Christians *should* do and not just how biblical people *were* to act.[1] As Old Testament scholar Walter Kaiser has noted, "Even more influential in the eclipse and collapse of Biblical law for modernity have been the twin developments of critical methods of Bible study and liberation/feminist theologies and hermeneutical systems."[2]

Pursuing a unified biblical ethics poses certain challenges. Some of the challenges to biblical ethics emerge from putting various texts in Scripture in competition, and then ruling in favor of one. For instance, Cosgrove points to Francis Wayland (1796–1865), who

[1] See Bartholomew, "Introduction," in *A Royal Priesthood?*, 7 (see chap. 1, n. 2).

[2] Walter Kaiser, "New Approaches to Old Testament Ethics," *Journal of the Evangelical Theological Society* 35, no. 3 (1992): 292.

argued that the issue of slavery in the Old Testament held less revelatory weight than what was taught in the New Testament.[3] This approach seems to work, but it in fact undermines the authority of the entire Bible by introducing distinctions between what counts as "more revelatory." In short, oftentimes the quickest way "out" of a particular challenge is not a way out at all, but a wrong turn that creates problems later. As Kaiser has noted, culture becomes the controlling factor.[4]

In what follows, we will address three types of challenges and explore how a unified biblical ethics might initiate responses to them. First, the coherency challenge, like the example above, argues that the differences between the texts are so great that a unified biblical ethic is impossible and therefore an external authority must determine what, if anything, can be taken from Scripture. Second, the trajectory challenge traces supposed development not only within the biblical texts but even beyond them, plotting differences in the texts along a trend of development and improvement that we must continue even today in the church. Third, the relevancy challenge insists that today's ethical challenges are so different from what the Bible actually addresses that Scripture's voice is basically irrelevant.

The Coherency Challenge

The first challenge to biblical ethics as we have discussed it so far is the challenge of coherency. For many scholars, the Bible contains a variety of ethical voices, which we cannot ultimately reconcile.[5]

---

[3] See Cosgrove, "Scripture in Ethics: A History," 22 (see chap. 1, n. 49).

[4] See Kaiser, "New Approaches to Old Testament Ethics," 293.

[5] A light version of this idea: "the Bible does not portray a single, unitary ethical vision. We see multiple visions, each connecting people with

Extreme versions of this echo the Marcionite heresy from the early church. In essence, Christian theologian Marcion of Sinope argued that the Old and New Testaments were really about two different gods—a vengeful God in the Old Testament and a gracious God in the New Testament. For Marcion, the choice was easy. The God of the New Testament was clearly better. A similar move appears attractive in ethics—the New Testament really shows us a more evolved, purer ethic than the Old Testament does. Or so it might seem.

The coherency challenge today does not typically extend as far as Marcion did. Some Bible scholars go even beyond this, stripping divine authority from various texts, claiming that they are more about the historical situation or historical background than they are a Word from God to his people. For those who hold this perspective, the issue is not so much whether there are two separate divine beings in the Bible but whether there is a divine voice discernible at all in the Bible. Due to the supposed lack of coherence, the idea is advanced that most of these moral issues must simply be time-bound attempts at morality; no coherence exists to unite the texts or to make clear how we are impacted by them today in any authoritative way.

This coherency challenge does not emerge only in scholarly circles, however. Sometimes Christians and churches implicitly make the charge that the Bible lacks a coherent moral voice by only applying to limited portions of the text on moral issues. Many Christians tend to exalt the teachings of Jesus or the writings of Paul in a way that implies the ethics of the Old Testament has little

---

God, who has made the world and will remake it." Gosnell, *The Ethical Vision of the Bible*, 30 (see chap. 2, n. 2). Gosnell and I likely disagree more on how to define "unitary," while others cited in this section will drive a much more significant wedge into the variety we see.

for Christians today. We must strike a balance here—clearly Jesus's teaching is something unique (though never contrary to the Old Testament), and Paul does speak clearly and truly about many ethical issues. But Jesus and Paul did not see themselves as lacking coherence with the rest of God's Word but as fulfilling it and applying it to new covenant people.

We will look at two types of this challenge. First, some scholars argue for no coherency at all in the biblical text. Second, others attempt coherency by using the idea of progressive revelation, a doctrine that most Christians hold to but that can be applied in ways that ultimately undermine the coherency of the entire Bible. Let's look at these types in turn.

No Coherency

Some biblical scholars and ethicists argue that there is no coherence to speak of in the Bible's treatment of ethics. As Bruce Birch and Larry Rasmussen put it, "The canon does not speak in a single voice."[6] We see this in a few ways.

On one hand, some scholars argue that the Bible is simply a collection of disconnected religious writings, and the only ethics we can talk about are the ethics of the particular writer or group that the writer represents. This perspective leads to narrower and narrower views of ethics, and it tends to remove any sense of normativity from the Bible. We can know scattered truths about what particular ancient groups such as the Israelites *thought* was right and wrong, but that tells us nothing, according to this way of thinking, about how we should live or act today. It is all incoherent.

---

[6] Birch and Rasmussen, *Bible and Ethics in the Christian Life*, 174 (see chap. 1, n. 5).

The charge of incoherency extends beyond Old Testament versus New Testament themes. Some see so much incoherence within the New Testament itself that they believe Christians must pick and choose what to listen to. As Shelly Matthews says, "Christians who reach for the Bible to argue for sensible gun control often build their arguments on the New Testament. Does that work? Yes and no. The New Testament has potential to support a peaceful ethic but also contains verses that can be used in support of violence. Only an approach that recognizes the New Testament's double message and chooses its peaceful strands over its violent ones can achieve that goal honestly."[7] Later in the same essay, she puts it even more bluntly: "Questions about how to place biblical teaching with respect to modern justice debates cannot be answered simply by relying on biblical criticism to peel away misconceptions and misinterpretations and pull out the kernel or pristine ethical truth. The Bible is multilayered and multi-voiced; it can be used in support of justice but also in support of injustice."[8] Several notable elements emerge. First, Matthews sees such incoherency in the Bible that Matthews believes we cannot even speak of a consistent New Testament ethic. We must note this point because she is honest about the perspective that divides the text. Some Christians might feel comfortable dividing the Old Testament and the New Testament in this way, but the knife does not stop cutting there! And if we expect something consistent in the New Testament, why not in the Old Testament as well?

---

[7] Shelly Matthews, "This Sword Is Double-Edged: A Feminist Approach to the Bible and Gun Culture," in *God and Guns: The Bible against American Gun Culture*, ed. Christopher B. Hays and C. L. Crouch (Louisville: Westminster John Knox, 2022), 93.

[8] Matthews, "This Sword Is Double-Edged," 104.

Second, Matthews charges anyone who finds unity in the New Testament on violence as being guilty of lying, employing a dishonest method to emphasize peace. (Who knows what her charge would be against those who choose violent strands over peaceful strands.) Operating behind the scenes, Matthews's own presuppositions about the superiority of these "peace strands" supposedly allows her to deal "honestly" and achieve her goal. But why reserve honesty for those who fail to see the consistency that is present in the text when understood within God's overall work? Third and finally, we see the ultimate conclusion of Matthews's incoherency challenge: ultimately, anyone can use the Bible however they want, and no analytical or interpretive tools can adjudicate between those readings. It is presumed, therefore, that contemporary values, which Matthews brings to the text, are the only way to save the Bible. The Bible becomes a tool of ideologies, and we can only hope that the right one wins out. This quandary represents the culmination of the coherency challenge—ultimately, coherency must be supplied, and we had better hope that the right people supply it.

On the other hand, some scholars argue that there might be some coherence within specific groups of texts, but ultimately there is no unified voice. Charles Cosgrove goes so far as to say, "The Bible also carries within itself codes of oppression; it, too, is a bearer of ideology."[9] Later he provides a key for interpreting such texts: "God is against ideology, that is, opposed to those cultural norms, values, institutions, etc. that serve the interests of the more powerful at the expense of the less powerful."[10] Coherence is found in being opposed to the powerful, in all cases, full stop. Still others

---

[9] Charles Cosgrove, *Appealing to Scripture in Moral Debate: Five Hermeneutical Rules* (Grand Rapids: Eerdmans, 2002), 91.

[10] Cosgrove, 109.

throw up their hands altogether. As Keck puts it, "It is not evident that the New Testament has any ethics to be studied."[11] Indeed!

These positions vary in the degree of incoherence they see, but they each end up with little to no coherence to speak of, and certainly little on which contemporary Christians can build. One way, however, at least to attempt to build coherence comes through using the doctrine of progressive revelation and applying it to the Bible's ethics.

Progressive Coherency

The doctrine of progressive revelation is that God unveils portions of his plan as time goes on and more details emerge through Scripture as time passes. Many Christians have found this understanding to be a helpful way of seeing the cohesion of the Bible, especially with regard to what God reveals about his plans in Jesus Christ. While some might read the Bible as though Jesus's life, death, and resurrection were sort of a Plan B or Plan C for God—with something like the Old Testament sacrificial system as Plan A—progressive revelation reminds us that God has not changed his plan for redemption but has mercifully revealed it more clearly as time has gone on.

One way to address the challenge of the coherence of the Bible's ethical vision relies on a modification and appropriation of the doctrine of progressive revelation. According to this version, the morality of the Old Testament no longer applies because it was a more primitive form than the morality of the New Testament. In other words, God progressively revealed moral truth in a way that makes

[11] Leander E. Keck, "Rethinking 'New Testament Ethics,'" *Journal of Biblical Literature* 115, no. 1 (1996): 3.

previous moral truth obsolete because it is not as advanced as what is revealed in the New Testament. Progression, for this approach, means discarding the old simply because the new is newer.

This position requires careful attention, because it is similar to other positions but based on different claims. Progressive coherence does not rely on the covenants—or the storyline of the entire Bible, or the difference between God's old covenant people (Israel) and his new covenant people (the church)—to make sense of the unified ethical vision of the Bible. Instead, the most important piece is progress, the fact that the later moral vision is given priority over the older moral vision simply because it is revealed later in Scripture. This approach fails to take seriously the unified ethical vision of the Old Testament because it fails to incorporate that vision into an overall vision of God rooted in the character of God worked out in the plan of God.

Conclusion of the Coherency Challenge

The coherency challenge takes many forms. It is rooted in a common enough observation: the Bible was written over hundreds of years by many different authors. Without a divine author, the coherency challenge has no real answer. We see that in those who deny any coherency at all—they are working with a human text and are therefore unable to see anything like coherency.

But we also see something of a divine authorship problem with other views of coherency. Those who lean on something like progressive revelation to overcome incoherency often do so in a way that minimizes God's purposes and plan in what he was communicating early in the Bible and how that part of the story continues to bind and motivate Christians today. For example, we can too readily identify Old Testament ethics with an earlier "stage" of revelation and then effectively ignore it rather than receive it, rightly interpreted, within the broader narrative of the Bible.

The approach we have explored so far demonstrates a different response to this challenge. Rather than surrender coherency, or take a progressive approach to it, we must instead see that the narrative of Scripture—not simple progress—provides coherency to all ethical material in the Bible because all ethical material in the Bible is connected to God's revealing himself and his will to his people. Dealing with the text "as it is" enables us to celebrate the diverse ways that biblical writers express God's will.[12] Understanding the particular covenant, and the particular task of God's people at that particular time, lends a more promising way to see coherence and to make sense of Scripture's one voice, God's voice.

The Trajectory Challenge

In the pursuit of holiness, some contemporary Christian ethicists have jettisoned Scripture's authority based on perceived deficiencies (often related to Paul). Others claim the Bible's primacy while moving beyond it in other ways. One particularly seductive method is what some call a "trajectory hermeneutic." This approach employs cultural analysis in a peculiar way. In short, they argue that the lesson we should take from the ethics of the New Testament is how the New Testament writers were even more, say, egalitarian, than their neighbors. Charles Cosgrove noted this tendency in modern approaches to biblical ethics. As he puts it, "by assuming that the revelation of morality in Scripture is from the primitive to the more enlightened, they plotted an evolutionary trajectory that pointed

[12] See Robert W. Wall, "Introduction: New Testament Ethics," *Horizons in Biblical Theology* 5, no. 2 (1983): 50.

beyond the limited egalitarian vision of the apostles (such as Paul) to perfect equality of the sexes as God's ultimate will."[13] Others have seen this tendency to be captive to the culture. In fact, "More common has been a primary identification with the larger society, with its problems and possibilities, and a corresponding measure of alienation from the church, especially as a major locus of moral interest. Ethical perspectives reflecting a strong identification with the larger society derive their moral substance from normative understandings integral to the basic institutions of society."[14] In short, when the primary concern is the broader culture, it is no surprise when the values of the culture supersede the values of the Bible, erasing them.

The task of the Christian today, in this view, is not only to obey what the Bible says but to follow the Bible's trajectory, pressing to be even more progressive than our current culture. Many Christian ethicists today take this for granted.[15] Rather than do what the Bible says, we should go beyond it, or perhaps even toss portions of it aside if they do not fit our definition of "revelatory."[16] For some, this approach includes the sort of biblical narrative we have explored, but the goal is to extend the narrative in new, transformative, surprising ways.[17] If women were the first witnesses to the resurrection, not only should we see this as an indication of their equality with men as bearers of truth, we should press beyond this

---

[13] Cosgrove, "Scripture in Ethics: A History," 22 (see chap. 1, n. 49).

[14] Thomas W. Ogletree, *The Use of the Bible in Christian Ethics* (Philadelphia: Fortress, 1983), 182.

[15] For example, see Lisa Sowle Cahill, "Gender and Strategies for Goodness: The New Testament and Ethics," *Journal of Religion* 80, no. 3 (2000): 442–60.

[16] See again Cahill, "Gender and Strategies for Goodness," 456, where Cahill notes this tendency on the part of some feminist biblical scholars.

[17] See, for example, Birch and Rasmussen, *Bible and Ethics in the Christian Life*, 28–29.

and be sure to champion women in the pastorate. In some cases, this same trajectory is then taken and applied to sexual ethics. By making this move, Christian ethicists claim to submit to the Bible's authority, but they actually make cultural definitions of equality, of goodness, and of right into a framework that they use to manipulate the Bible's clear moral witness to holiness.

Perhaps the most fully developed example of a trajectory hermeneutic is William Webb's seminal work, *Slaves, Women, and Homosexuals: Exploring the Hermeneutics of Cultural Analysis.* In fact, Webb himself offers "trajectory hermeneutic" as an optional name for his approach, though he prefers "redemptive movement hermeneutic,"[18] a choice we will revisit later. Webb proposes this approach because he thinks that too many come to the Bible in the wrong way, practicing "isolated reading." For Webb, an "isolated reading" is "a reading of [the Bible's] words in isolation from the spirit-movement component of meaning which significantly transforms the application of texts for subsequent generations."[19] There are a couple important features to note here. First, Webb is not talking about a Holy Spirit–guided reading. As evidenced by the lowercase "spirit," the redemptive spirit is identified neither with the biblical storyline nor with the work of the Spirit. It is a vague sense of "redemption" and "liberation," left undefined. Second, pay attention to what drives significant transformation here—not God but a loosely defined, lowercase "spirit." Application transforms over time, relative to subsequent generations and their perception of what this "spirit" might mean. Allowing Webb to further explain his principle will make clearer what drives this transformation.

---

[18] William Webb, *Slaves, Women, and Homosexuals: Exploring the Hermeneutics of Cultural Analysis* (Downers Grove, IL: IVP, 2001), 31.

[19] Webb, 34.

Webb simplifies his model using what he calls the "X—>Y—>Z Principle":

> Within the model below, the *central position* (Y) stands for where the isolated words of the Bible are in their development of a subject. Then, on either side of the biblical text, one must ask the question of perspective: What is my understanding of the biblical text, if I am looking from the perspective of the *original culture* (X)? Also, what does the biblical text look like from our contemporary culture, where it happens to reflect a better social ethic—one closer to an *ultimate ethic* (Z) than to the ethic revealed in the isolated words of the biblical text?[20]

He puts the stakes brusquely: "What we should live out in our modern culture, however, is not the isolated words of the text but the *redemptive spirit* that the text reflects as read against its original culture. In applying the text to our era, we do not want to stay static with the text (Y). Rather, we need to move on, beyond the text, and take the redemptive dimension of those words further to a more redemptive level (toward an ultimate ethic, Z)."[21] In pursuing this line of argument, Webb takes several missteps. First, he relies on a false dichotomy. He argues that someone must either follow his method or assume everything in the Bible is transcultural,[22] which ends up muzzling the Bible's redemptive spirit.[23] Second, at the same time, he acknowledges the difficulty of discerning this redemptive movement. It is delicate, he admits, and

---

[20] Webb, 31.

[21] Webb, 33.

[22] See Webb, 52.

[23] See Webb, 45.

requires listening "for how the text sounds within its various social contexts."[24] He mentions the foreign context (ancient Near East), the domestic context (social setting of the modern reader), and the canonical context (the movement across biblical epochs).[25] Third, Webb subtly alters the nature of Scripture in his model. He casts the Word of God as "isolated" and in need of reinterpretation, with reconstructed ancient cultural values and ethics playing a leading role. This move not only puts the reconstruction of the ancient context into the driver's seat for determining meaning; it also denigrates what the Bible actually *is*. This model does not treat the Bible as operating within a divine economy of a gracious God redeeming and guiding his people by the work of the Son in the power of the Spirit. Instead, the Bible is a trove of information and data, one that requires some extra work to get any value from. Trajectory hermeneutics sacrifice the character and nature of the holy text by isolating it from the God who speaks and transforming it through supposed "spirits" discernible by paying more attention to ancient and modern culture than the text itself.

This example of the trajectory hermeneutic also makes clear that modern scientific and social scientific hypotheses enjoy greater authority than traditional Christian interpretations of the Bible. Yet, by allowing a large role for a "social-science component," Webb opens the door to inverting the text entirely. Theologians have long used the idea of "accommodation" to make sense of how God speaks to his creatures, but Webb allows for social-scientific data to determine what in the Bible is "relative" and what is absolute.[26] Perhaps something the Bible treats seriously was simply God

---

[24] Webb, 53.

[25] See Webb, 53.

[26] Webb, 64–65.

accommodating his people because social science had not been invented yet. Further, Webb says that extrascriptural criteria are "no less weighty" than criteria from the biblical text in determining how ethics may need to develop beyond what the Bible says.[27] This position completely ignores the noetic effects of the fall because it does not account for the fact that we might misunderstand whatever real-world data we are seeing and trying to interpret. Webb's trajectory hermeneutic makes it possible, if not likely, that the fallen mind might manipulate social science to reinterpret biblical truth, making it culturally relative.

Like many approaches that emphasize cultural issues, Webb gets the first question wrong. He claims that the question "Should I go *against* my culture or move *with* my culture?" is "the crucial question" in wrestling with ethical issues.[28] Placing this question first forgets that our first question should be some combination of "What does God say?" and "Will I obey?" Putting culture first causes all sorts of problems. Webb defines a "cultural component" as follows: "those aspects of the biblical text that 'we leave behind' as opposed to 'take with us' due to cultural differences between the text's world and the interpreters' world as we apply the text to subsequent generations."[29] Clearly, the problem emerges—no text should fit this definition. We should not leave any aspect of the biblical text behind because of cultural differences. Rather, our interpretation must be rooted in what God has revealed about the redemptive narrative of Scripture, that particular command's place in it, and our place in it. It has nothing to do with our culture or the culture of the Bible. Yet Webb uses

---

[27] Webb, 17.

[28] Webb, 22.

[29] Webb, 24.

this rubric to define the entire hermeneutic: "We need to ask the question, Which components within Scripture are cultural and which are transcultural?"[30] This question demonstrates problematic assumptions about the nature of the text and its moral claim on Christians.

Let's return to Webb's choice of a name for his hermeneutic. He calls it a "redemptive movement" hermeneutic because he wants to show that "the derived meaning is internal, not external, to the biblical text."[31] A valid concern, indeed, but Webb's "redemptive movement" is disconnected from the Bible's redemptive story. In short, Christians most frequently use "redemptive" in a particular way—tied to God's redeeming plan in Jesus Christ. However, Webb uses a more general definition, one approaching a kind of situational ethics. He states that the most important part of the application process is "to engage the redemptive spirit of the text in a way that moves the contemporary appropriation of the text beyond its original-application framing. A sense of the biblical or redemptive spirit can be obtained by listening to how texts compare to the broader cultural milieu and how they sound within the development of the canon. When taking the ancient text into our modern world, the redemptive spirit of Scripture *is the most significant dimension with which a Christian can wrestle*."[32] In other words, cultural comparison based on vaguely articulated values (such as "justice") become the benchmarks for interpreting God's commands in Scripture. Webb uses "redemptive" not to mean "made sense of in light of God's specific work in Christ" but "oriented to cultural analysis of abstract values."

[30] Webb, 29.

[31] Webb, 31.

[32] Webb, 30 (emphasis added).

To Webb's credit, his text itself seeks to demonstrate how delicate this interpretation is, and how various issues come through the process differently. The book is not titled *Slaves, Women, and Homosexuals* because he thinks those three issues all come out the same. He argues against Christian adoption of homosexuality based on his model.[33] However, his model sows the seeds for even his own interpretation to be labeled hopelessly backward and anti-redemptive. We can see this type of tendency in other examples of a trajectory hermeneutic.

Another popular example of this way of thinking relies on labeling parts of the Bible "patriarchal" and insisting that the trajectory the Bible identifies is away from patriarchy, and therefore we must take it even further. Bartholomew puts it bluntly: "A strong strand of thought today argues that the Bible is a deeply ideological book with unhelpful nationalistic, patriarchal, ethnicist and sexist elements."[34] As Shelly Matthews explains, "A key aspect of feminist biblical interpretation is the observation that the Bible was written in a patriarchal—or *kyriarchal*—context and that these aspects of the Bible must be identified, critiqued, and rejected for the sake of our salvation."[35] Two elements merit careful attention here. First, the Bible is lumped broadly under a "patriarchal context," which is obvious enough but also not particular enough to help in any way. There are all sorts of patriarchal contexts, and articulating them more carefully might aid in understanding the Bible. But for Matthews, the simple "observation"

---

[33] See Webb, 39. "The Christian community must continue its negative assessment of homosexual behavior and restrict such activity within the church, even if society at large does not."

[34] Bartholomew, "Introduction," in *A Royal Priesthood?*, 11 (see chap. 1, n. 2).

[35] Matthews, "This Sword Is Double-Edged," 104.

requires identifying elements for the purpose of rejection—not further understanding. Second, Matthews's critique has no logical conclusion but the complete rejection of the Bible *as a whole.* If the Bible was written in a context and that context must be rejected, there is no way to transplant the text to a new context for writing. In short, if the context of the Bible's writing is this big of a problem, there will be nothing left after the identification, critique, and rejection.

Matthews continues the critique by pointing to broad positive principles that serve to determine which texts matter and why. The only thing that serves as a basis for evaluation of the texts is a set of broad principles, "including community benefit, human flourishing, and the all-important principle of neighbor love."[36] For her, these ideas allow interpreters to determine what needs rejecting and what can be advanced and applied. But remember, any biblical concept—even community benefit, human flourishing, and neighbor love—would have been written about and expressed in a patriarchal context. It is unclear how these concepts, emerging from the same texts and contexts, can be reliable. Again, we see that this trajectory challenge ultimately identifies contemporary cultural values as transcendentally good and authoritative and able to evaluate and even reject elements of the Bible.

Another place we find a trajectory argument about how to interpret the biblical text centers on the notion of God's purposes but leaves "purposes" vague and gives a lot of power to whatever we understand those purposes to be. For example, David Instone-Brewer argues, "When we read the Bible, we are looking over the shoulders of people living a few thousand years ago, for whom it was originally written. The law of Moses was

---

[36] Matthews, 106.

revolutionary to them because it challenged them to live different lives. It didn't immediately transform them into a fully egalitarian society with a social-benefit system and legally protected human rights, *but it did point them in that direction and pushed them as far as possible*."[37] He pushes this perspective further, using it to argue that Paul "probably wanted to sweep away other laws, too, because he regarded women, slaves, and non-slaves as completely equal. But instead, he advocated voluntarily keeping the status quo for the sake of the gospel (Gal 3:28)."[38] In other words, Paul wanted to go further than he did, but he dialed it back since the church was not ready for it.

Instone-Brewer leaves little room for confusion in his advocacy for continuing on the Bible's trajectory rather than obeying what the Bible, properly interpreted, actually says. He concludes:

> God's laws in the Bible constantly pushed humanity forward in order to change them for the better—in areas of punishment, equality, and care of the oppressed. God's law changed people as much as they changed at the time. This means that some details of God's laws changed when society and circumstances changed. The unchangeable nature of God's law lies in the underlying principles and purposes: the most valuable things on earth are people, not commodities. This is the unchanging ethical principle of the Bible. God supremely loves and values people, and his law teaches every generation to do the same.[39]

---

[37] David Instone-Brewer, *Moral Questions of the Bible: Timeless Truth in a Changing World* (Bellingham, WA: Lexham, 2019), 6 (emphasis added).

[38] Instone-Brewer, 9.

[39] Instone-Brewer, 9–10.

This lengthy quote demonstrates the pieces of the trajectory hermeneutic—things change, God is always pushing people further, and every generation must do the same.

Pieces of this example ring true, which is why it is such a challenge. We do notice differences in what the Bible says about issues, and we sense that it would be inappropriate to follow through on things like stoning adulterers. However, the idea that God's purposes are as general as Instone-Brewer claims sets us up to enthrone our cultural values as what God must have been driving at all the time. Notice that this approach does not center on glorifying Jesus as the purpose of the Father, but on "people are the most valuable." It is not the case that people are *not* valuable but that the Bible roots this conclusion in creation and in the work of Christ, not in generalities.

A briefer example relates to Paul's mention of homosexuality in Romans 1. Cosgrove seeks a purpose behind this text that pushes Christians today to move beyond the rule against homosexuality. He writes, "Paul probably regards the prohibition of homoerotic behavior as an absolute rule. Under the rule of purpose, however, we are to treat the justification for this rule as weightier (for us) than the rule itself."[40] He goes on to explain that the real purpose was to avoid idolatry and unbridled passion in a world that misunderstood homosexuality as unnatural. Therefore, the point is to avoid these things. Cosgrove even grants that reconstructing the purpose of this example might be difficult to do, in which case "one should not use Romans 1 as a guide in developing a Christian position on contemporary homosexuality(ies)."[41] On the one hand, we might be able to reconstruct a purpose that helps us identify a trajectory to

---

[40] Cosgrove, *Appealing to Scripture in Moral Debate*, 38.

[41] Cosgrove, 44.

follow. On the other hand, it might be too difficult to reconstruct a purpose, in which case we set aside Paul's words altogether from our contemporary attempt to understand the morality of homosexuality! This, despite the work of scholars who have shown that "there is clear, strong, and credible evidence that the Bible unequivocally defines same-sex intercourse as sin" and "there exist no valid hermeneutical arguments, derived from either general principles of biblical interpretation or scientific knowledge and experience, for overriding the Bible's authority on this matter."[42] For those who buy into a trajectory hermeneutic, all such evidence can simply be lined up and dismissed in light of supposed "purposes" that may or may not be reconstructible.

A final example puts the issue quite starkly. John Rogerson argues that the Old Testament in particular requires a clear movement away from what the text actually says. For him, laws are expressions of human sensitivity, not the divine will. God is always working through human sensitivity to moral matters, and as that sensitivity improves, so do moral expectations. As he puts it, "In short, the Old Testament does not lay down timeless laws or principles that express God's blueprint for creation. It teaches us that *God approves what moral sensitivity at its best holds to be right*."[43] He continues to argue that this sensitivity is not static; instead, "it must change in accordance with deepening insights, and part of this change is to be brought about from the pressure provided by the imperative of redemption."[44] Others move in this direction via

---

[42] Robert A. J. Gagnon, *The Bible and Homosexual Practice: Texts and Hermeneutics* (Nashville: Abingdon, 2001), 37.

[43] John Rogerson, *Theory and Practice in Old Testament Ethics*, ed. M. Daniel Carroll R. (New York: T&T Clark, 2004), 17 (emphasis added).

[44] Rogerson, 19.

the language of "virtue," arguing for the need to "update" actual notions of right and wrong but rooting them in supposed "virtues" the Bible does confirm.[45] Clearly, for scholars such as these, biblical ethics requires nearly as much correction of what the Bible actually says as application of what it says![46]

Conclusion of the Trajectory Challenge

The trajectory challenge emphasizes transformation beyond what the Bible itself sets out. As Birch and Rasmussen say, "In both the OT and the NT, *imitatio Dei/Christi* does not imply that we simply try to do what God or Jesus have done. . . . But through the testimony of Israel and the early church in the witness of biblical texts, we can enter into the reality of God and Christ in ways that shape and form our character as moral agents and communities. We enter into the life of God *in ways that transform our own lives as moral agents and communities, and that transform the broader social structures of which we are a part*."[47] The problem is that once the Bible is removed as the ultimate authority and instead placed earlier in the trajectory, the transformation proposed becomes completely unmoored and unaccountable. O'Donovan wrestles with a similar viewpoint, which he calls the "paradigm model," and concludes this way: "The paradigm-model will not do what it is often thought to

---

[45] For more on this path, see Lúcás Chan, S.J., "Biblical Ethics: 3D," *Theological Studies* 76, no. 1 (2015): 118.

[46] Ultimately, this approach finds difficulty actually dealing with ethical issues. For instance, Cahill struggles to make any sense of divorce. See Lisa Sowle Cahill, "Gender and Strategies for Goodness: The New Testament and Ethics," *Journal of Religion* 80, no. 3 (2000): 459.

[47] Birch and Rasmussen, *Bible and Ethics in the Christian Life*, 31 (emphasis added).

do. It will not deliver us from the need to admit that some prescriptions two thousand years old can claim us."[48] Indeed.

The Relevancy Challenge

The third challenge to the unified voice of biblical ethics is the relevancy challenge. On the most extreme end, some argue that the Bible is so rooted in its time that it cannot be relevant at all to ethical matters in the modern world. As Oliver O'Donovan summarizes this challenge: "At the heart of the current uncertainty is the question of time: can a value-judgment which was true, or a prescription which was appropriate, many centuries ago, still be appropriate today?"[49] This perspective tends to diminish the divine authority of Scripture, arguing instead that it is merely a historical record of religious thoughts that sometimes inspires religious thought and practice today.

From a more moderate perspective, the challenge of relevancy is not leveled in a total sense but in a limited one. This limited sense still ultimately undermines and destroys the text, however. Some might argue that though the biblical text contains truth, its historical circumstances are so different that its moral perspectives have no bearing at all on how we should think about and respond to issues today. This challenge is similar to the trajectory challenge, but it instead sees no connection between the biblical commands and contemporary Christian witness. The idea is not, "Let's work from antiquated biblical sexual ethics to what a 'love ethic' looks like today" (as a trajectory hermeneutic might) but instead, "Ancient descriptions of killing a child in the womb just are not at all what abortion in modern culture is, so we can discard the text entirely." Sure, the Bible might have

---

[48] O'Donovan, "Towards an Interpretation of Biblical Ethics," 72 (see chap. 5, n. 7).

[49] O'Donovan, 69.

something to say about sexuality or the value of unborn life, but it is not relevant to the challenges we experience today.

While there might not be many examples of this relevancy challenge put in such direct words, it underlies many approaches to ethics, and even Christian ethics, today. When we ignore the biblical text, we give in to the relevancy challenge, tacitly accepting that our challenges are too different from the Bible for the Bible to be useful. We can quickly forget that the Bible's relevance is not settled by cultural approximations to our own culture but by divine communication of the Triune God. Spelling out some examples of this challenge will help us to notice this tendency.

One example of the relevancy challenge comes in the discussion of sexual ethics, and homosexuality in particular. For some scholars, a simple argument can be made: the tradition did not understand what homosexual desire really is, so the moral statements with regard to homosexuality are not addressing what we see today in our culture. As David Gushee puts it:

> The ancient tradition of historic Christianity appears never to have had a moral category to describe homosexual persons, that is, persons of persistent and enduring same-sex rather than opposite-sex sexual/romantic attraction or orientation—because the entire concept of orientation is relatively recent. Nor did Christianity have a concept by which people might identify themselves in terms of that attraction pattern, such as under the contemporary labels "straight" or "lesbian," or "gay" or "bisexual." . . . Such identity labels are also quite recent, and then continue to proliferate.[50]

---

[50] David P. Gushee and Glen H. Stassen, *Kingdom Ethics: Following Jesus in Contemporary Context*, 2nd ed. (Grand Rapids: Eerdmans, 2016), 265.

Trace the logic carefully here. We have a new concept, orientation, which means something like "persistent and enduring attraction." The Bible, it is presumed, could not be talking about this concept, and therefore its clear moral statements against homosexuality are not relevant. The assumption seems to be that those moral statements are applicable only to "straight" people. Something like, "If you are normally attracted to the opposite sex, it is wrong to pursue homosexual action, but if you are persistently attracted to the same sex, then the Bible does not speak to you on this issue." A strange logic train, for sure!

Two problems emerge here. First, this perspective on the relevancy of biblical terminology often fails to demonstrate that the supposed "new terms" are actually new. Even if many of the ancient examples of homosexuality involve males who have wives but use younger men for sex, it does not follow that ancient texts like the Bible could not speak to that specific distortion of the creation order while also connecting to the overall rejection of God's order. Just because the examples from the surrounding culture trend in a certain direction does not mean that the biblical terminology is narrowly limited to those contexts.

Second, even if the terms are new in important ways, the conclusion of the argument does not necessarily follow. It runs something like this:

> Premise A: Contemporary terms about homosexuality refer to persistent orientation.
>
> Premise B: Biblical terms about homosexuality do not refer to persistent orientation.
>
> Conclusion: Therefore, biblical perspectives on homosexuality do not apply to what we refer to in our day with the term.

Did you notice the hidden third premise? It would be something like this:

> Premise C: If biblical terms do not refer to persistent orientation, then persistent homosexual orientation is not subject to the biblical sexual ethic.

The problem with this hidden premise, besides the fact that it is not stated, is that it does not necessarily follow from the first two. Our contemporary language might highlight persistent orientation in a way that the biblical terminology does not (I am only conceding this for the point of this argument; I do not think the language is as clean as these arguments make it sound). However, why should we assume that biblical language could be biblical language and still applicable to modern challenges, even if we emphasize different elements of the moral problem? In other words, that the Bible does not dwell on persistent orientation does not mean the prohibitions of homosexuality do not apply. The biblical terminology could emphasize some other aspect, besides persistence, and still apply. In fact, it is helpful to think of the biblical argument as rooted in something that is against nature, against the way God made men and women. Whether a man or a woman has a persistent aversion to that order or not, it is still a problem. Another example of the need for nuance and careful application of biblical truth arises in cases of psycho-physiological additions to alcohol or any other substance. Just because we have a more detailed understanding of the physiology of such sins does not mean that we recategorize them completely. They do not cease becoming sins simply because we see how complicated and deep human brokenness in fact is! We still need forgiveness; God still promises wholeness and redemption.

Another way to articulate the Bible's lack of relevance is to claim that something vague like "principles" matter, but not the specifics of the text. For instance, Charles Cosgrove claims Christian ethicists have settled on a consensus that the Bible shouldn't be used "prescriptively," in that its moral rules are not our moral rules. The consensus is that the basic values and principles apply, but not the rules.[51] Even if this represents a consensus, how do we determine what the principles are, or the values, or how they apply? This shift away from rules, rooted only in a general acknowledgment of "values and principles," leaves the text with little authority or use. Instead, we should root any sense of the Bible's "prescriptive" use in something the Bible itself provides: a narrative of God's work in calling a people to himself and to be his witnesses.

One more way to articulate this challenge of relevance is to demote the Bible and its authority to the authority of the church. This route is the one Birch and Rasmussen take, insisting over and over again that the community is the locus of moral formation, the community helps interpret the Bible (even in ways that seem to contradict its original meaning), and the community figures out how to make the Bible relevant because it is not relevant on its own. The Bible is unique, but not on account of itself. Instead, "This uniqueness is not inherent in the Bible as one piece amidst the corpus of the world's literature. It appears only when the location for the shaping of moral character and conduct is the church. It is the faith community that claims a special place for the Bible as part of the confession of its own identity."[52] When the Bible is submitted to the community and gets its authority not from its divine origin but from its community use, it is no surprise that the community must make it relevant. It certainly has no relevance on its own if it has no divine authority.

---

[51] See Cosgrove, *Appealing to Scripture in Moral Debate*, 5.

[52] Birch and Rasmussen, *Bible and Ethics in the Christian Life*, 151.

In the end, the relevancy challenge is fairly straightforward. Some make this point by trying to distinguish between "Christian ethics" and "biblical ethics," with the former being more holistic, and the latter being strikingly limited. Briefly: "biblical ethics cannot be synonymous with Christian ethics [because] biblical communities did not confront some of the moral issues and social forces that shape our lives today. The Bible does not begin to imagine some of the moral issues that are part of modern life in the twenty-first century."[53] Often such arguments not to make the two synonymous serve to jettison the Bible in order to set a different standard or guideline.

Conclusion

All three of these types of challenges—coherency, trajectory, and relevancy—pose problems for any biblical ethics that hears a unified voice speaking through the entire Bible. Part of the impetus for these challenges has been the supposed difference between the Bible's world and our own. But this difference is often overstated, denying the important fact that the most important aspect is that God is present and speaks here, in his Word. As John Webster helpfully puts it:

> Much of the labour of hermeneutically oriented revisionist theology is expended upon the task of negotiating some kind of correlation between the strange biblical world and the realities of contemporary experience. But both strategies are rendered superfluous if the hermeneutical situation is defined not out of the paradigm of historical remoteness

[53] Birch and Rasmussen, *Bible and Ethics in the Christian Life*, 6.

> but out of the presence of God as Word. What determines the hermeneutical situation, and thus the acts of human agents in that situation, is the presence and activity of Jesus, the 'revealedness' of God.[54]

In reality, these challenges start off on the wrong foot, so of course they lead to the wrong destinations. The wrong problems are in view. Webster's reflection on this fact provides a fitting end to considering these challenges:

> If sophisticated hermeneutical theory fails to persuade, it is largely because, in the end, it addresses the wrong problems, and leaves untouched the real difficulty with reading Scripture. That difficulty . . . is spiritual and therefore moral; it is our refusal as sinners to be spoken to, our wicked repudiation of the divine address, our desire to speak the final word to ourselves. From those sicknesses of the soul, no amount of sophistication can heal us.[55]

Indeed.

---

[54] Webster, *Word and Church*, 69 (see chap. 1, n. 17).

[55] Webster, 109.

7

The Practice of Biblical Ethics

Pursuing biblical ethics in this manner is no easy task. Someone unfamiliar with the Bible cannot simply search and find a few interesting verses and extrapolate a "biblical" position. There is no process that you can lay out, step-by-step. We cannot define the mechanism, at least not in a totalizing way. Sometimes we approach such challenges by saying something is "more of an art than a science." That sentiment might ring true here with biblical ethics, so we will expand on it a bit. It is difficult to talk about "art" today because of the various notions people have about art—what counts as art, whether someone is simply born with artistic talent or can develop it, and so on—it might help to think of an early time period. In early periods, artists grew through a combination of apprenticeship and what today we might consider plagiarism—simply copying great artists. You developed as an artist by working closely with a master because doing so enabled you to pick up the types of things that could easily be instructed as well as the types of habits and sentiments that we develop subconsciously. Copying great artists gave a young artist the opportunity not only to see what was worth emulating but also to develop the ability to make similar brushstrokes, to see similar subjects as worthy, and so forth.

We are in a similar place when it comes to developing biblical ethics. Biblical ethics is a practice that we enter into in ways similar to artists of centuries past. There are practices that can help us develop as biblical ethicists, even if we cannot put everything down into a step-by-step process or catalogue every verse into a particular ethical issue and render verdicts. Instead, we will pursue two ways that we develop as biblical ethicists—through what I call "preparatory practices" and "crisis practices." We will start with the preparation, not because we always have that luxury in real life but because we certainly do in a book.

Preparatory Practices

Paying Attention to the Text

The first practice that builds and sustains a whole-Bible biblical ethics is simple: regular, focused attention paid to the text of Scripture. Nothing replaces regular exposure to the entire canon. In short: read the Bible, again and again. We must practice this way both because of what ethics is and because of what the Bible is. Ethics is more than just finding answers to questions when the questions confront us (though we will deal with that later in this chapter). Samuel Wells gets it right: "Christian ethics is not about helping anyone act Christianly in a crisis, but about helping Christians embody their faith in the practices of discipleship all the time."[1] A biblical ethics that focuses on the Bible's unified voice and seeks that voice through regular, systematic immersion in the text of the Bible better prepares us to see ethics in just this way.

This attention to the text must be first to the Bible as a whole, not merely to portions of it that we find helpful in moral reflection. This sustained attention to the whole Bible can be difficult because we long for simplicity in preparing for ethical crises. Responding to the moral crises we face in contemporary society, pastor Jonathan K. Dodson approvingly incorporates the assertion that points to the Sermon on the Mount as the greatest moral document of all time.[2] While this assertion might be true in a sense—never mind helpful at the start of a book focusing on the contemporary relevance of the Beatitudes—it can also cultivate a dangerous attitude. We are all drawn to the (false) promise that mastering a handful of texts might make everything simpler; mastery might provide wisdom. Unfortunately, we always want a smaller handful than the handful God has given—his Word, Genesis through Revelation.

Now, the problem is not finding particular texts or groups of texts uniquely helpful or clear, but in separating them and failing to interpret them in light of the entire counsel of God. I am sure Dodson would agree, as he demonstrates by drawing other biblical texts into his explanation of the Beatitudes throughout his book. But we must nevertheless watch ourselves, for preparatory practices related to the text of Scripture must center on the whole of

---

[1] Samuel Wells, *Improvisation: The Drama of Christian Ethics* (Grand Rapids: Brazos, 2004), 15.

[2] See Jonathan K. Dodson, *Our Good Crisis: Overcoming Moral Chaos in the Beatitudes* (Downers Grove, IL: IVP, 2020), 13–14.

Scripture before the parts, and then, the parts directed toward the whole.

Recall what was said about strip-mining in chapter 1. To extract valuable minerals from inside the mountain, the mining company blows the top off of it, exposing the valuables and making them more easily accessible. This practice might be convenient for the miners, but it decimates the mountain and surrounding area. We can do the same thing with the Bible when we fall into the idea that the Bible "contains" certain data points that we have to extract and then refine or sharpen or apply. This temptation is not always indulged but can follow from advice like this: "Our knowledge, then, with which to evaluate ethical issues is *gathered from* Scripture."[3] The very language that we use sometimes betrays this attitude toward Scripture. We might think we gain information from it, but we have destroyed so much in doing so that we actually need to make sense of the information we have mined.

This regular, sustained attention to the Bible itself is due to the nature of the Bible. What the Bible actually *is* draws us into it in this manner. As theologian John Webster helpfully describes the Bible, "Though its genres are widely divergent . . . , the Bible as a whole is *address*, the *viva vox Dei* [the very words of God] which accosts us and requires attention. God's address is interceptive; it does not leave the hearer in neutrality, or merely invite us to adopt a position vis-à-vis itself and entertain it as a possibility. It allows no safe havens; it *judges*."[4] This quotation highlights several aspects of the

---

[3] Walter C. Kaiser, Jr., *What Does the Lord Require?: A Guide for Preaching and Teaching Biblical Ethics* (Grand Rapids: Baker, 2009), 10 (emphasis added).

[4] Webster, *Word and Church*, 75 (see chap. 1, n. 17). For a thorough exploration of the various genres of the Bible and how they impact

text that require the type of attention we are discussing here. First, the whole Bible is *to* God's people. The voice of God speaks—God "accosts" us, as Webster puts it. He grabs our attention. Second, the address of the Bible leaves us no neutral ground; it offers no safe invitation. The *judgment* of the Bible can be avoided, or at least softened, if we pick and choose some texts and ignore others or if we isolate texts outside of the biblical redemptive context. In other words, avoiding the Bible as the very *voice* of God might allow us to isolate "moral texts" from other texts, but doing so can act to evacuate the power of the texts, of God's Word, and instead open up the interpretive process to being co-opted by contemporary spirits of the age.

This attention to the text will also enable us to find help in surprising places. For instance, many do not think of the Psalms as ripe for ethical reflection. Gordon Wenham argues otherwise: "The psalms have much to say about behavior, about what actions please God and what he hates, so that anyone praying them is simultaneously being taught an ethic. Those who use the psalms as prayers are often not aware of this aspect, but I will argue it is one of the most potent forms of ethical indoctrination. It happens in all kinds of worship situations."[5] We might not turn to Psalms immediately if confronted with an ethical challenge, but biblical ethics developed by sustained attention to the whole of Scripture will pick these elements up.

What applies to the Psalms extends beyond to other unlikely texts. If Christian ethics is ultimately rooted in a redemptive story

---

faithful preaching and application of the text, see O'Donnell and Ryken, *The Beauty and Power of Biblical Exposition* (see chap. 5, n. 6).

[5] Gordan J. Wenham, *Psalms as Torah: Reading Biblical Song Ethically* (Grand Rapids: Baker, 2012), 2.

with God as the main actor and if we hear God's unified voice throughout Scripture, then the first preparatory practice is to listen to this voice regularly.

Holy Spirit, Illumination, and Christ

A second practice, or rather one that goes along with the practice of textual attention, is calling upon and relying on the Holy Spirit. Any faithful approach to biblical ethics needs to acknowledge the role of the Holy Spirit. The doctrine of illumination reminds us that we need God's help to hear and understand God's Word properly, and the Holy Spirit's role is to assist in that attempt. But the Holy Spirit does not fit in here only because of his aid in the work of interpretation. We also see why the Spirit's role fits particularly well for a unified biblical ethic centered on the story of redemption accomplished in Christ.

While we will not expand this section into an entire doctrine of the Holy Spirit, it helps to remember what Jesus said about the Holy Spirit's role when he promised the Spirit's coming. On the night of his betrayal, Jesus said, "If you love me, you will keep my commands. And I will ask the Father, and he will give you another Counselor to be with you forever. He is the Spirit of truth. The world is unable to receive him because it doesn't see him or know him. But you do know him, because he remains with you and will be in you" (John 14:15–17). A little later, he continued with another reference to the work of the Holy Spirit: "When the Counselor comes, the one I will send to you from the Father—the Spirit of truth who proceeds from the Father—he will testify about me. You also will testify, because you have been with me from the beginning" (John 15:26–27). We see from these passages that there are a few roles Jesus promised that the Holy Spirit would fulfill.

First, the Holy Spirit is called the Spirit of truth, and the Father gives the Spirit in connection with Jesus's statement about obedience. The Holy Spirit helps Jesus's followers to know and obey the truth. Second, we see that the Spirit testifies about Jesus. The Spirit's role is to point to Jesus Christ, to testify about him, to help his followers know the truth and obey it. How does this apply to preparatory practices for biblical ethics? The model we are following insists that Jesus Christ is the climax of the entire Bible and that all of the Bible, including its ethics, revolves around the story of redemption that Jesus accomplishes. This orientation fits closely with the way Jesus talks about the Spirit here in John 14 and 15. If the Spirit indeed does what Jesus promises here, this fact fits well with the type of Christ-centered interpretation that a unified biblical ethics requires and inspires.

Community

Christians prepare for the practice of biblical ethics by paying attention to the text under the power of the Holy Spirit. But this act is not an isolated affair; rather, Christians do this in community with other believers.

Communitarian emphases have enjoyed greater popularity in recent years due to many related factors. On one hand, philosophers have emphasized the social location of knowing—we all come to know what we come to know in particular places related to particular people. On the other hand, various forms of collectivism have gained some level of prominence politically, even within democratic, independent societies. In short, many people agree that communities matter, that communities shape us, and that we are more than just a bunch of individuals who choose to relate in various ways.

However, Christians pursue biblical ethics in community not because of these philosophical or sociological arguments but because of what the Bible teaches about the church as a body. In 1 Corinthians 12, Paul described the church as a body with many members, members with different characteristics, strengths, and roles, but members invested in the good of the body (1 Cor 12:12–31). God has not created merely a bunch of individuals, but a body. That body finds its expression in each local congregation. Christians recognize the importance of the body in interpreting and applying the Bible because God intends to sanctify us within this context, within the body of which we are a part.

Some theologians have picked up ideas of theatre performances to illustrate the role of the community in the task of interpreting and applying the Bible. For instance, ethicist Samuel Wells compares ethics to improvisational theatre. In his mind, the church does not so much follow a script—even a lost script—as it does pursue faithfulness shaped by the Bible. As he puts it, "The Bible is not so much a script that the church leans and performs as it is a training school that shapes the habits and practices of a community."[6] Wells himself draws on such theologians as N. T. Wright, Gabriel Fackre, Paul D. Hanson, Bernhard W. Anderson, and others.[7] The community is vital because the task is faithful "improvisation."

Theologian Kevin Vanhoozer has developed a similar idea for Christian theology as a whole. Drawing on the work of theologians such as Hans Urs von Balthasar and others, he writes, "Doctrine is a response to something *beheld*—beheld not theoretically but,

[6] Wells, *Improvisation*, 12.

[7] See Wells, 225n11.

as it were, theatrically: a *lived* performance."[8] He develops this further in another volume, where he explains, "To learn Christian doctrine only from textbooks rather than from participating in the communion of saints is like reading Shakespeare but never encountering a live performance: it may be informative, but it is rarely *trans*formative. Disciples best learn how to *practice* doctrinal truth through *paideia*, an apprentice-based pedagogy that involves following the examples of (i.e., imitating) others who are further along."[9] For Vanhoozer, our beliefs are not merely something we learn from a book or from talking about them; rather, we learn embedded within communities of worship, communities of faithful practice—for worship is certainly more than but not less than faithful life.

Both of these approaches and explanations demonstrate the importance of Christian community in the task of biblical ethics. The community of faith needs the canon of Scripture, and while individuals can certainly develop an understanding independently, the nature of God's work is centered in the church, which has a continual conversation with the Bible. As one scholar explains, "In the on-going conversation between community and canon, it is the canon which bears the Word of the Lord and it is the canon which corrects and bids new Israel to repent and turn to God—a 'prophetic interplay.'"[10] This dynamic interplay is significant as the church, located within God's ongoing story, comes to understand the story and live rightly within it.

---

[8] Kevin Vanhoozer, *The Drama of Doctrine: A Canonical Linguistic Approach to Christian Theology* (Louisville: Westminster John Knox, 2005), 17.

[9] Kevin Vanhoozer, *Faith Speaking Understanding: Performing the Drama of Doctrine* (Louisville: Westminster John Knox, 2014), 7.

[10] Wall, "Introduction," 53 (see chap. 6, n. 12).

Crisis Practices: Bringing Questions without Distorting the Text

As noted at the beginning of this chapter, we do not always have the luxury of preparation. In the previous section, we highlighted how biblical ethics is properly rooted in careful, prolonged attention to the Bible itself as a whole, under the guidance of the Holy Spirit, enmeshed in Christian community. But what about when we find ourselves with a particular ethical question, one pressing upon us, often without our choosing? These questions might come from our own life situations or from those around us, or just from what we see going on in the world. How do we bring these questions to the Bible for ethical insight?

First, we must acknowledge that our questions might lead us to distort the text. We can cause this distortion in several ways. For one, we might rush through the process, forcing texts into our preconceived notions or positions. Our hearts are deceitful, after all, so even as we bring our questions to the text in times of urgency, we should do so in a way that recognizes and makes room for the textual attention, the reliance on the Spirit, and the wisdom of the church community that we have covered in preparatory practices.

Second, we can gain wisdom from following a straightforward plan that can help us search, find, and listen to God's voice in Scripture. With the proper precautions, we can formulate a simplified approach for bringing questions to the Bible. For example, C. Ben Mitchell proposes a straightforward procedure for finding ethical guidance in the Bible. He highlights five main steps: First, pray for divine illumination. Second, define the ethical issues or problems. Third, clarify the issue to be examined. Fourth, glean all scriptural data on the issue. Fifth, study the scriptural instruction carefully.[11] This procedure moves forward logically, with clear focus on the text. When we are pressed for answers, it can help prevent us from distorting or silencing the text. Two cautions to observe, however. We must not underestimate the degree to which our definitions of the ethical issue or problem might dictate what we find relevant in the biblical text. Second, we must always keep in mind that the Bible is more than "data" and that in removing that data from the Bible, we are in danger of losing the very narrative and theological context that gives it the ethical sense we need.

While bringing our questions to the text, we must also resist the temptation to consider our question so new that the Bible does not speak to it at all, or that the Bible only speaks to it in a limited way. Oliver O'Donovan recognizes this temptation, explaining, "The problem-oriented approach to moral questions, on the other hand, finds itself constantly unable to get off the ground though failure to agree about the relevance of this or that piece of Biblical material."[12] As we have seen throughout this book, when we take the whole Bible into account, we not only realize the proper narrative and theological context in which to understand individual ethical statements; we also see the way God's commands and character draw us into a contemporary story of redemption.

After we emerge from our "crisis practices for biblical ethics"—or dilemma ethics—we should find ourselves drawn back to the preparatory practices we explored first. These preparatory practices lead to moral formation, to habits of thought and behavior

---

[11] See C. Ben Mitchell, *Ethics and Moral Reasoning* (Wheaton, IL: Crossway, 2013), 95.

[12] O'Donovan, "Towards an Interpretation of Biblical Ethics," 78 (see chap. 5, n. 7).

grounded in Scripture and illuminated by the Holy Spirit. Ideally, we do not turn to biblical ethics only when we have a particular question. Sometimes we have to, and we must do so carefully and prayerfully, but the task of understanding the Bible and finding ourselves within the Bible takes more than any method or list of steps can adequately cover.

But how might this look in real life? How do we bridge particular concerns or challenges to the biblical narrative? I have saved this for late in the book because we all must resist allowing pressing questions and the desire for practicality to prevent us from paying careful attention to what is eternal—God's Word. But we can now begin this important and practical task. Let's look at technology as an example.

Christians recognize that technological advances provide new opportunities and challenges for living a faithful Christian life. Personal devices such as laptops, tablets, and smartphones open up a previously unimaginable ability to access information and to communicate across vast distances. The Bible certainly speaks to such things, in multiple ways. If we bring the simple question of whether it is permissible to use such technology, we might find some simple and straightforward texts about the goodness of community or about the danger of sins such as anger and lust, which the digital environment can spur in different ways. But if we stop at "these tools are good if we use them for X and bad if we use them for Y," we miss the ways the broader biblical story speaks into and informs a biblical response to our times. We miss it because we can easily gloss over the types of community, care, and human flourishing that the Bible points toward in the fullness of salvation in Christ.

If we simply go to a sample of isolated texts, we are in danger of interpreting those texts in light of our cultural priorities instead of within the story of redemption that God is accomplishing. As I have argued elsewhere, broader Christian themes such as the Sabbath, the need for silence and solitude, and the significance of meaningful human work all weave throughout the biblical narrative and inform a biblical response to technology.[13] Each of these themes connects not only to individual commands or texts but also to the broader narrative of redemption. Even when confronted with the challenges of modern technology, we must do the hard work of seeking biblical formation of our view of the human problems that technology can solve, the ones that it cannot solve, and the ultimate need for God's work and redemption in all things.

Conclusion

Toward the start of our journey in this book, I encouraged you to resist the strip-mining approach to biblical ethics. When we come to the Bible with our ethical questions, we must resist the urge to blow the top off, grab what we can, and run away, leaving ruins behind us. Instead, we always seek to remember that the Bible is not a text that we handle; rather, it is God's very Word, one of the gracious means by which God handles *us* as he promises to cleanse us by the washing of his word (Eph 5:26). God's consistent voice speaks here, as God's gracious hand works to sanctify those who have placed their trust in the Son. Biblical ethics, like sanctification, is ongoing and regular. It is not relegated to the crises or applied by pulling out some relevant verses. Hearing God's

---

[13] See Jacob Shatzer, *Transhumanism and the Image of God: Today's Technology and the Future of Christian Discipleship* (Downers Grove, IL: IVP Academic, 2019), 172–75.

unified voice in biblical ethics requires a lifetime of careful, obedient, Spirit-empowered and church-rooted reading, rereading, and re-rereading of God's Word.

Even as we finish this book, the work of biblical ethics does not finish, but only ever continues.

FOR FURTHER READING

There are many helpful volumes on biblical ethics, volumes that reward a careful and thoughtful reading. The list below is not exhaustive; rather, it is just where I'd go from here.

Bavinck, Herman. *Reformed Ethics: Created, Fallen, and Converted Humanity*, ed. John Bolt. Grand Rapids: Baker, 2019.

Brock, Brian. *Singing the Ethos of God: On the Place of Christian Ethics in Scripture.* Grand Rapids: Eerdmans, 2007.

Gosnell, Peter W. *The Ethical Vision of the Bible: Learning Good from Knowing God.* Downers Grove, IL: IVP Academic, 2014.

Hays, Richard B. *The Moral Vision of the New Testament: A Contemporary Introduction to New Testament Ethics.* San Francisco: HarperOne, 1996.

Jones, David W. *An Introduction to Biblical Ethics.* Nashville: B&H, 2013.

Kaiser, Walter C. Jr. *What Does the Lord Require?: A Guide for Preaching and Teaching Biblical Ethics.* Grand Rapids: Baker, 2009.

McQuilkin, Robertson and Paul Copan. *An Introduction to Biblical Ethics: Walking in the Way of Wisdom*, 3rd ed. Downers Grove, IL: IVP Academic, 2014.

Tyra, Gary. *Pursuing Moral Faithfulness.* Downers Grove, IL: IVP Academic, 2015.

Vanhoozer, Kevin. *Faith Speaking Understanding: Performing the Drama of Doctrine.* Louisville: Westminster John Knox, 2014.

Wells, Samuel. *Improvisation: The Drama of Christian Ethics.* Grand Rapids: Brazos, 2004.

Wright, Christopher J. H. *Old Testament Ethics for the People of God.* Downers Grove, IL: IVP Academic, 2004.

ACKNOWLEDGMENTS

This book would not exist if not for the imagination and friendship of Jason Thacker. Jason took an offhand comment I made leading a doctoral seminar, developed an idea for this series, and invited me to write this volume on biblical ethics. He has also provided a keen revision and editing eye, meaning that he is responsible for this book's *being* and its being *better* than it would have been. All weaknesses of course are mine. Ben Mitchell has also shaped me and this book in many ways. Ben's mentorship and friendship have remained a consistent joy for me over the last fifteen years or so. Ben provided the first round of feedback on my rough draft, and he also gave me a place to stay for a short writing retreat that enabled me to finish the second draft. Thanks also to Michael McEwen, the editorial team at B&H Academic, and the help of their anonymous reviewers and editorial process.

I've had the complicated privilege of learning from several accomplished ethicists. A privilege, obviously, because of their care in teaching me; a complicated one, due to the various ways they (we!) all disagree. I'm thankful to have studied ethics with David Gushee, J. Daryl Charles, Ken Magnuson, M. Therese Lysaught, and D. Stephen Long.

I'm grateful to have found my academic home at my alma mater, Union University, where I am blessed to serve with so many gifted colleagues. My dean, Ray Van Neste; provost, John Netland; and president, Dub Oliver, have each supported me in various ways.

In the end, my family provides the foundation of support that starts and sustains projects like this one. Thank you, Keshia, Zeke, Jack, Mona, and Lena, for every day.

SUBJECT INDEX

A

abortion, 128
Abrahamic covenant, 56–59, 62
Abram/Abraham, 44–45, 52–53, 56–58, 61–62, 65, 70, 78, 104
Adam, 12, 15, 37–45, 53–57, 61, 74, 76
Anderson, Bernhard W., 142
art, 33, 135–36

B

Balthasar, Hans Urs von, 142–43
Bartholomew, Craig, 3, 42, 47–49, 122
Bauckham, Richard, 27
Beale, Greg, 37–38
Beatitudes, 86–87, 137
Bible
  authority of, 4–8, 108–9, 126–28
  broad principles within, 123
  community through, 141–43
  distortion of, 144
  diversity within, 96
  ethical challenges and, 98–101
  ethical responses and, 98–101
  feminist interpretation of, 122
  Holy Spirit–guided reading of, 117
  illumination of, 140–41
  images within, 11–13
  incoherency of, 110–13
  isolated reading of, 117
  judgment of, 139
  meaning communication within, 99
  nature of, 138
  overarching story of, 27–28
  overview of, 7–10
  part in relation to the whole interpretation, 101–5
  patriarchy of, 122–23
  patterns within, 10–11, 17–18
  paying attention to, 136–40
  persistent orientation and, 131
  prescriptive use of, 132
  progressive coherency of, 113–14
  rules within, 29–30
  studying practices of, 101–2
  symbols within, 8, 10–12
  temptations regarding, 145
  truth communication within, 7–8
  typology in, 14–17
  uniqueness of, 132
  whole-Bible ethics of, 97–98
biblical counseling, 2

biblical ethics
Christian ethics versus, 133
in the Christian life, 25–26
coherency challenge of, 108–15
crisis practices of, 144–47
economic angle for approaching, 75–76
incoherency and, 110–13
intersection of, 18–25
overview of, 2–5
practice of, 135–48
preparatory practices regarding, 136–43
progressive coherency and, 113–14
relevancy challenge of, 128–33
social angle for approaching, 75–76
strip-mining approach to, 26
theological angle for approaching, 75
trajectory challenge of, 115–28
biblical justice, 81–82
biblical label, 1
biblical preaching, 1–2
biblical theology, 2, 8–10, 97
Birch, Bruce, 110, 127, 132
blessings, 56–58, 65
bow (weapon), 102–3
Brock, Brian, 25
Burridge, Richard, 97–98

C

Calvin, John, 20
ceremonial law, 60
Christian ethics, 4–5, 25–26, 68, 73, 78, 83, 94, 129, 133, 136–37, 139
Christian life, biblical ethics in, 25–26
Christian morality, 72
church, 3, 6, 9, 14, 21, 24, 26, 48, 65, 82–83, 85–87, 90–92, 95, 101, 108–9, 114, 116, 122, 124, 127, 132, 142–44, 148
civilization, 36
civil law, 60
coherency challenge, 108–15
collectivism, 141
commands, 18–19, 21, 23, 32, 36–37, 43, 59–60, 71, 84, 99, 102, 121, 128, 140, 145, 147
community, 4, 58–59, 64, 77, 79, 90–92, 94, 96, 101, 122–23, 132, 141–44, 146
"context is king" concept, 101–3
Copan, Paul, 5
Cosgrove, Charles, 24, 107, 112, 115, 125, 132
covenants
with Abraham, 56–58
creation, 53–54
with David, 61–62
God's kingdom through, 52–53
with Moses, 58–61
new, 63–65
with Noah, 54–56
overview of, 51–52
creation covenant, 53–54
creation/creation story, 12, 24, 28–39, 41–43, 47–55, 57, 62, 65–66, 74, 76, 78–79, 90–91, 125–26, 130
creation mandate, 36–37
creatio prima, 35
creatio secunda, 35
cross, 13, 46, 48, 81, 90–93, 97
culture, 6, 23–24, 29, 33, 51, 53–54, 103, 108, 116, 118–21, 128–30

D

David (king), 15, 45, 53, 61–62
Davidic covenant, 61–62
Davis, Ellen, 80
death, 40, 46–47, 55, 71, 88, 90, 97, 103, 113

deontological ethics, 23
dilemma ethics, 25, 145
direction, 42–43, 50
disciples, 84, 143
disease, 49–50
disobedience, 39–43, 58–88
divine authority, 109, 128, 132
divine authorship, 114
Dodson, Jonathan K., 137

E

emotivism, 22–24
ethical egoism, 23–24
ethical relativism, 23, 93
ethics, task of, 6–7, 18–19, 85. *See also* biblical ethics
Eve, 38–43, 45, 54, 76

F

Fackre, Gabriel, 142
faithful love, 71–72
faithfulness, 45, 61, 71–74, 86, 91, 142
fall, the, 30, 39–44, 51, 62, 120
flood story, 12–13, 41, 44, 54–56
fruit of the Spirit, 86

G

garden of Eden, 37–41, 43
Gentry, Peter, 14–15, 52–53, 56–57, 62, 64
God
- character of, 21
- creation as temple of, 37–38
- as creator, 30–39
- holiness of, 81–83
- as Judge, 80–82
- law and, 21
- purposes of, 123–25
- relationship with, 28
- sovereignty of, 15, 32–35
- voice of, 9, 105, 139

Goheen, Michael, 42, 47–49
"go out" command, 104
Gosnell, Peter, 28, 109
grace, 41, 43, 61, 64
grass, 33–35
Great Commission, 84
Gushee, David, 129–30, 151

H

Hamilton, James, 9–11, 15–16
Hanson, Paul D., 142
Hays, Richard, 4, 90–93
healing, 49–50
Herod the Great (king), 15
holiness, 21, 59, 82–83, 86, 101, 104, 115, 117
holy living, 87, 89
Holy Spirit, 21, 25, 41, 47, 64, 82, 84, 86–87, 90, 104, 117, 119, 140–41, 144, 146, 148
Holy Spirit–guided reading of the Bible, 117
homosexuality, 102, 122, 125–26, 129–31
human freedom, 35
human sexuality, 102–3
hypermasculinity, 102–3

I

idolatry, 88, 125
image of God, 53–54, 74, 76–78, 85
inaugurated eschatology, 65
incoherency, 110–14
Instone-Brewer, David, 123–25
international treaties, 52, 59
isolated reading of the Bible, 117
Israel/Israelites, 4, 13, 16, 45–46, 53, 57–65, 69, 71, 74–76, 78–79, 81–83, 90, 101, 110, 114, 127, 143

J

Jesus
- ascension of, 47
- covenants and, 63–64
- creation and, 35–36
- death of, 46

illumination through, 140–41
imagery usage by, 13
obedience of, 90
patterns and, 18
as the promised Seed, 40, 43–46
redemption through, 44–49
resurrection of, 46–47
return of, 47–48
suffering of, 92
typology of, 15–17
unification through, 97
virtue teaching by, 73
Jones, David, 4–5, 69
Joseph of Egypt, 45
justice, 72–74, 80–82

K

Kaiser, Walter, 107–8
kingdom of God, 21, 43, 46–49, 52–53, 63, 82–83, 101
kingship, 61–63

L

labeling, 1, 122
land, as Old Testament theme, 78–80
law
Christians and, 19–21
classification of, 59–60
human reception of, 34
human sensitivity and, 126
imposing of, 33
nature's reception of, 33–34
Old Testament, 101
purpose of, 20–21
uses of, 20
violation of, 71–72
laws of nature, 32
Lemos, T. M., 102–3
love, 92–94

M

Marcionite heresy, 109
Marcion of Sinope, 109
Matthews, Shelly, 111–12, 122–23
McQuilkin, Robertson, 5
Mitchell, C. Ben, 144
moral beliefs, 6
morality, 6, 22–24, 28, 72, 109, 113, 115, 126
moral law, 5, 60, 69
moral posture, 96
moral reasoning, 6, 22–24
Mosaic covenant, 19, 58–62
Moses, 11, 13, 15–16, 24, 45, 58–61, 123

N

natural law, 24–25
new covenant, 16, 21, 62–65, 69, 73–74, 110, 114
new creation, 37, 55, 79, 90–92
New Testament ethics
focal images within, 90–92
key texts within, 83–94
love in, 92–94
Noah, 12–13, 41, 44, 52–57, 62
Noahic covenant, 54–56

O

obedience, 38, 59, 64–65, 68, 85, 90–92, 104, 141
O'Donnell, Douglas Sean, 98–99
O'Donovan, Oliver, 99–100, 104, 127–28, 145
Old Testament
ethics, 4, 74–83
holiness theme within, 82–83
image of God theme within, 76–78
justice theme within, 80–82
key texts within, 68–74
land theme within, 78–80

P

paradigm model, 127
patriarchy, 122–23
Paul (apostle), 18, 35–36, 41–42, 85, 87–89, 97, 109–10, 115–16, 124–26, 142

peace, 45, 63, 86, 112
persistent orientation, 130–31
Peter (apostle), 13, 89
photosynthesis, 34–36
poetry, 7–8
priesthood, 16, 59
progressive coherency, 113–15
Promised Land, 16, 45, 57, 62, 78

R

Rae, Scott, 6, 22, 82
Rasmussen, Larry, 110, 127, 132
redemption, 10, 30, 41–52, 63, 65, 75, 89, 93, 95, 98, 100–101, 103, 113, 117, 126, 131, 140–41, 145, 147
relevancy challenge, 108, 128–33
reproduction, 32–33
righteousness, 20, 47, 63, 87–90
Rogerson, John, 126
Roman Christians, 85
Rosner, Brian, 9
rulership, 53–54
Ryken, Leland, 98–99

S

sacrificial systems, 11, 16, 58, 113
salvation, 13, 21, 47–49, 57, 63, 65, 88, 97, 122, 146
sanctification, 69, 85–88, 104, 147
Satan, 39–40, 49
Saul, 45
Schreiner, Thomas, 19–20
seeds, 32–33
sentimentalism, 71–72
Sermon on the Mount, 16, 86, 137
sexual ethics, 117, 128–32
sin, 5, 13, 16, 36, 39–46, 48–49, 56–58, 62–64, 88–90, 93, 103, 126, 131, 146
slavery, 16, 108
Solomon (king), 45
sonship, 53–54
structure, 5, 42–43, 50, 60
suzerainty treaty, 70

T

technology, 146–47
temple, God's creation as, 38–39
Ten Commandments, 3, 5, 58–60, 68–71
theatre performances, 142
Tower of Babel, 41, 44, 56
trajectory challenge, 108, 115–28
Tyra, Gary, 72–73

U

universalization, 99–100, 104
utilitarianism, 22–24

V

Vanhoozer, Kevin, 142–43
Verhey, Allen, 5–6, 47, 96
violence, 31, 44, 102, 111–12
virtue ethics, 23–24, 83–84

W

Wayland, Francis, 107–8
weapons, 102–3
Webb, William, 117–22
Webster, John, ix, 10, 133–34, 138–39
Wells, Samuel, 136–37, 142
Wellum, Stephen, 14–15, 52–53, 56–57, 62, 64
Wenham, Gordon, 139
wisdom, 36, 45, 137, 144
Wolters, Al, 30–34, 36, 42, 50
women, significance of, 116–17
Wright, Christopher J. H., 4, 74–75, 78–80, 82
Wright, N. T., 94, 142

X

X→Y→Z Principle, 118

Z

Zimmermann, Ruben, 77